THE CONTAGIOUS WITNESS

Exploring Christian Conversion

Ron Crandall

ABINGDON PRESS
Nashville

THE CONTAGIOUS WITNESS
EXPLORING CHRISTIAN CONVERSION

This book is printed on recycled, acid-free paper.

Cataloging-in-Publication data is available from the Library of Congress.

99 00 01 02 03 04 05 06 07 08—10 9 8 7 6 5 4 3 2 1

MANUFACTURED IN THE UNITED STATES OF AMERICA

CONTENTS

PREFACE

How do people come to a vital Christian faith and a personal experience of God? What is the role of others who serve as agents of grace in that process? These are questions I have been asking for more than forty years.

God first became real to me at a summer church camp when I was fifteen. It was obvious in the moments and months that followed, maybe for some even painfully obvious, that I did not know much about how to be a Christian witness. But my life had been profoundly changed, and I deeply believed God intended for every person to discover the unsurpassed wonder and power of love that had touched my heart. I wanted to be an agent of God, a contagious Christian witness.

Most of us recognize some truth in Stephen Covey's observation that "in spite of how much we would like to, we cannot turn someone else's key. He must turn his own. Our greatest help to him is to turn ours."[1] In many ways Mother Teresa demonstrated the power of this approach as a Christian witness. But is it enough to simply live our own convictions? Often, rather than helping others come to their own life-changing experience of God, this kind of faith modeling only makes them feel they don't understand why religious people are such "do-gooders." In fact, unless we clarify that it is God's love in our hearts that motivates us to do what we do, and unless we can explain how others can find this same reality, we may be working against God's design for us to be carriers of the good news that this gift of "salvation" and new life is for *everyone*. What is the relationship between living an authentic life of faithfulness and telling others how they can come to know God and become the persons they were created to be? This is the question that prompted the research reported in these pages.

Chapter One attempts to clarify why the nature of God as Holy Trinity is critical to the meaning of the Christian gospel. Although

7

this may seem like theological gobbledygook to some readers who prefer the "practical" to the "theological," it is the conviction of this writer that to properly understand and experience God as Holy Trinity is to be freed for joyful Christian living and contagious witness. In these opening pages the rationale for the theme and the imagery of the book is established. To catch the "good infection," a metaphor for the life of salvation in Christ that I will use throughout this book is to become contagious for the glory of God.

Chapter Two shifts from examining the nature of God as Holy Trinity to combing the Bible to discover the heart of the contagion we are commissioned to carry. What is the gospel? Three strains of the good infection are traced through both testaments: (1) the glory of God, (2) the kingdom of God, and (3) the new covenant. Although the descriptive terminology varies some for each of these living threads, when taken together they reveal an almost DNA-like picture of the eternal triune life of God and help clarify how that life is able to be transferred to God's children. Divine love shaped for the human soul is the mystery revealed.

Chapters Three, Four, and Five take us from conceptual reality to experienced reality. Drawing on data contributed by more than ten thousand persons interviewed over the course of fifteen years,[2] Christian converts collectively tell their stories of how they came to experience the saving and transforming power of God at work in their lives. Chapter Three looks at the agents of contagion and the faith patterns of those who came to faith as children. Chapter Four examines the unique dynamics at work for those who came to trust in Christ when they were adolescents. Chapter Five shifts the scene to examine the faith journeys of those who catch the good infection as adults. The goal in each of these chapters is not merely to present data, but to better understand how we might be helpful to others as Christian witnesses.

The final chapter seeks to bring theology and research data together in order to discern additional lessons for all of us who as parents, friends, church leaders, and as entire congregations wish to become better carriers of the good infection, faithful and productive evangelists.

Evangelism begins with God, not with us. It begins with God's own nature and with God's activity. Any of us who dare to speak of the God who has met us and who can meet others are only able to do so because this is who God is and what God does. The God of the Bible and the God of Christian experience and Christian evangelism is uniquely and eternally personal. Thus, to bear witness to this God is always a deeply personal matter. Perhaps this is one reason why we sometimes avoid the opportunities for Christian witness that are granted us. Christian evangelism is not primarily teaching about ideas. Nor is it a market transaction that tries to close a sale. It is primarily a matter of deep soul sharing about why we believe in a personal God, the God of Abraham, Isaac, and Jacob; the God of Sarah, Elizabeth, and Mary; and ultimately, the God who is our Source, our Savior, and our Sustenance—Father, Son, and Holy Spirit.

May this God make us more contagious as we endeavor to reveal "Christ in us, the hope of glory"[3] and as we invite others to surrender their impoverished souls to God's Son and our Savior, Jesus, and thereby find in his Spirit all the wonders of amazing grace.

ACKNOWLEDGMENTS

I am deeply indebted to all of my students who labored to amass the data used in this book. More than six thousand hours of actual face-to-face interviews and another three thousand hours of processing the data from those interviews are represented in these pages.

It would be impossible to name all who have contributed, but I am particularly indebted to Eric Silver and to Doug Coone, who worked with me on this project for several years giving both technical guidance and serving as coordinators of the teams who processed the data.

Above all, I am grateful to my family for the way each one has been a gift of God to open my life to a greater understanding and experience of divine love. My prayer is that in some way I have likewise contributed to you.

And to you, Matthew and Joshua, I hope the record of God's activity recorded in these pages will encourage you to be faithful witnesses for your generation.

> One life to live, it will soon be past,
> Only what's done for Christ will last.

CHAPTER ONE

The Contagious God

"Contagious—capable of being transmitted, as from one person to another."
"God—the one Supreme Being, the creator and ruler of the universe."
— *Webster's Encyclopedic Unabridged Dictionary of the English Language*

"Will you or won't you...join in the dance?
—The Lobster, *Alice in Wonderland*

Who Is God and What Is God Like?

Such a question scatters a covey of fluttering answers rising from the underbrush. A myriad of images and understandings emerge. Even among those of us who consider ourselves "Christian" it doesn't take long in most conversations to discover that we don't all share identical "theologies" (God thoughts). Some would attribute these differences, whether large or small, to history and our various theological backgrounds and denominations. Others would say the differences are primarily cultural and reflect varying worldviews in place before a Christian view of God was added. Others would say the problem is simply a matter of lack of "maturity" or experience. Still others might categorize the differences more in the black-and-white issues of knowledge and ignorance, truth and fallacy, good and evil.

In reality, probably all of these factors have contributed to our differences. I easily recognize how each of these influences has shaped my own journey of faith and how I have undergone shifts, adjustments, and even "conversions" in my perceptions of God. In fact, it is precisely this realization that has given me courage to write this and attempt to describe God. Who would dare such a thing? Who can describe God except God? Exactly! And that must be our starting point: what God has already allowed us to touch, taste, see, and hear of the divine nature. Otherwise we are even worse off than the proverbial troop of blind men who attempt to describe an elephant by examining only the particular part each happens to be touching. I say even worse off, because we would be attempting to describe what is not only invisible but also "untouchable." Of course this is exactly the problem skeptics and religious agnostics believe we are facing. They would say everything we utter about God is only the blabbering of the blind who gropingly go about describing an invisible, untouchable, unknowable, and probably imaginary entity.

God's Self-Revelation

Although the primary purpose of this chapter is to examine God's contagious nature and not to offer a mini-course on divine revelation, a quick summary of some of the ways we know what we know about God might be helpful. So, what has God shown us or said to us that allows us to speak as those who "know"?

The God of Creation

It is easy to acknowledge that the most "natural" starting point in speaking about God is the creation itself. The psalmist wrote:

> When I look at your heavens, the work of your fingers,
> the moon and the stars that you have established;
> what are human beings that you are mindful of them,
> mortals that you care for them? (Psalm 8:3-4)

When God is recognized as the Creator of all that we can view, especially in this era when our "view" is literally being expanded to edges of the universe as well as to the subatomic level of "quarks" and "leptons," human beings are indeed strangely in "the middle" and rightfully in awe of the Mystery behind it all. God the Creator, who could and did initiate this awesome spectacle and who maintains it, is due every imagined ounce of respect and authority able to be generated by any creature. And if this Creator not only resembles an all-powerful Mind, but also a loving and compassionate Heart—as the psalmist believed—who cares for us in a very special way, an even more intimate response is called for than merely respect. In fact, it might best come forth as a song—a love song full of praise and adoration—as it did for the psalmist.[1]

A more contemporary hymn writer, Stuart Hine, penned it this way:

> O Lord my God! when I in awesome wonder
>   consider all the worlds thy hands have made,
> I see the stars, I hear the rolling thunder,
>   thy power throughout the universe displayed.
> Then sings my soul, my Savior God to thee;
>   how great thou art, how great thou art![2]

Actually, creation by itself does not produce this ability of a soul to sing "my Savior God to thee." Many who deeply appreciate the creation and who study it as scientists still feel hesitant to declare they know anything at all about the Mystery behind it—even if they "wish they could." In 1996, after suffering through months of cancer and facing death, Carl Sagan, the brilliant cosmologist and atheist confessed:

> I would love to believe that when I die I will live again, that some thinking, feeling, remembering part of me will continue. But as much as I want to believe that...I know of nothing to suggest that it is more than wishful thinking.
> I am satisfied with the mystery of the eternity of life and a glimpse of the marvelous structure of the existing world, together with the devoted striving to comprehend a portion, be it ever so tiny, of the Reason that manifests itself in nature.[3]

The Apostle Paul reminded his audience in Rome that there was a double message regarding God's self-revelation in creation: "For what can be known about God is plain to them, because God has shown it to them. Ever since the creation of the world his eternal power and divine nature, invisible though they are, have been understood and seen through the things he has made. So they are without excuse; for though they knew God, they did not honor him as God or give thanks to him.... Claiming to be wise, they became fools" (Romans 1:19-22).

Creation is a starting point for many of us. We can know *something* of God's nature through creation even as *something* can be known of any artist through his or her work. In fact, since we ourselves are part of the creation, there is good reason to believe that we could learn of God by looking within and examining ourselves. The evangelist Paul as he presented the gospel of God's revelation in Jesus Christ to Epicurean and Stoic philosophers in Athens, used this premise and reminded them:

> Then Paul stood in front of the Areopagus and said, "Athenians, I see how extremely religious you are in every way. For as I went through the city and looked carefully at the objects of your worship, I found among them an altar with the inscription, 'To an unknown god.' What therefore you worship as unknown, this I proclaim to you. The God who made the world and everything in it, he who is Lord of heaven and earth, does not live in shrines made by human hands, nor is he served by human hands, as though he needed anything, since he himself gives to all mortals life and breath and all things. From one ancestor he made all nations to inhabit the whole earth, and he allotted the times of their existence and the boundaries of the places where they would live, so that they would search for God and perhaps grope for him and find him—though indeed he is not far from each one of us. For 'In him we live and move and have our being'; as even some of your own poets have said, 'For we too are his offspring.' " (Acts 17:22-28)

Thus, as we grope for God, looking outward to the heavens and inward to the human soul, there is enough revealed to make us humble and grateful. However, the God of creation most often still seems as distant as the stars, and the God of nature as indifferent to human beings as the last flood or the next great wind or fire. Left without additional revelation, God's children can do no better than announce they believe, but terribly miss the mark when it comes to honoring the Creator with their lives, since God is largely still "unknown." Little that resembles the faith of the psalmist or that of the great hymn writers is found simply by celebrating nature and groping to find God. Something more is needed, and has been

16

given. God speaks and acts in history as well as in creation. This is the second level of revelation.

The God Who Speaks

Almost all the religions of the world have established mechanisms to listen to the voice of God. These vary from listening to "the still small voice within," which we often describe either as conscience or inspiration, to listening to specially designated prophets, seers, sages, and shamans either directly or through their writings. Perhaps this reveals again that we are all of one origin and "in him we live and move and have our being." However, what we "hear" through these various channels seems to lead to much more diversity than unity. Something is wrong.

Some would say God is not talking at all and we are only engaging in our own brands of religious hallucination. No one way of knowing God and God's will is better than another because in reality all of them are only human imaginations. None are really divine revelations. Probably all of us have harbored these thoughts at one time or another and wondered if there were any sure way of knowing what is true and what is not true about God.

Others would explain the problem by saying we are all limited in our ability to receive everything that God is communicating, and therefore our religions each have only a portion of the whole. This is why we need each other. Only when we come together, cooperate, and engage in truly open inter-religious dialogue will the complete message God is speaking be heard by any and all of us. This way of thinking assumes there are no real contradictions or mutually exclusive ideas involved in our "truths," rather we all have some "truth" but none of us yet has the whole "Truth." This is why there appears to be a problem. However, the problem will one day disappear when we reach the top of the mountain where our various paths will meet and we will understand completely. Until then, let us have charity toward one another and be faithful to as much as God has revealed to us.

There certainly are some attractive qualities about this approach. It especially appeals to those of us who recognize that we don't know it all, and that we don't particularly care to associate with those who act as though they do. There is a certain humility in this approach which is attractive to "enlightened" persons not only in matters of religion but in a whole multitude of issues. After all, even those things which we once were taught to be so sure of (Columbus discovered America; atoms are composed of protons, neutrons, and electrons; communists are God's greatest enemies; American presidents are models of wisdom and virtue—just to name a few) are now open to question or even proven to be obsolete. And, on the other hand, all of us hopefully have found that the prejudiced and even hateful stereotypes of persons from other cultures and religions were just that, and not at all helpful in making us "good neighbors"—an idea inherent in some form or another in all great religions.

But there are some problems with this approach as well. Is God really this poor at communicating? Is the God of order revealed in the creation the God of confusion revealed in the world's religions? Or are humans this poor at receiving divine revelation? Granted, the human receiver may not be perfectly in tune to the divine message, but even if the peripheral ideas of these diverse religions are allowed to coexist because they are seen as non-essentials, major differences remain in what is claimed as the nature, character, and purposes of God. Although it may at times seem "nice" and even prudent in today's pluralistic world to withhold judgment about the religious views of others (in part because few of us have ever really carefully examined our own), any optimism that this will eventually lead us to a deep and harmonious unity seems sadly blind to the facts. God cannot be both the author of order and the author of confusion, at least so the Bible claims.[4] And although it is possible to affirm some similarities in the basic moral guidelines set forth by many of the world's religions, it is not possible to harmonize their varying views of God's own nature. In fact, this is where the greatest disparity is found. So where does that leave us?

A third approach to resolving the problem is to recognize that there are various levels of revelation. There is general revelation such as that discussed above under the category of the God of creation. There is also a kind of remnant revelation built into every human being as one created to be a child of God. This remnant of God's mark on all humanity creates both the rudimentary voice of our conscience and a hunger, perhaps even a "groping," to find God and discover the meaning of our lives. In every society there are some who hunger and thirst after God, truth, and meaning more than others. These spiritually sensitive souls seem more attuned to "right and wrong" and to "good and evil." In addition to seeking answers for themselves, they have a strong desire to help others overcome life's struggles, sin, and pain.

A long list of such spiritual leaders could be offered, ranging from Socrates and Plato in the West to K'ung-Fu-tzu (Confucius) and Siddhartha Gautama (Buddha) in the East. Each of these offered his own list of insights and truths, along with spiritual directives for those who would seek to understand the mystery of life. Interestingly enough, however, of these four only Buddha and Confucius spawned lasting "religions," and neither of them claimed to know anything about God. Both were agnostics and claimed no knowledge of God. This is not to say they were "false teachers," but only to say that they were not "true messiahs." They offered much that inspired generations to live more orderly and moral lives, and perhaps to the degree their models of morality were faithful to the remnant voice of God within their souls, they were divinely inspired. But their voices offer little help to those of us who wish to hear more directly from God. For this kind of voice we need to turn to those sources rooted in another history and recorded in the Bible, the third level of revelation.

The God of the Bible

The God of the Bible is the unique, personal Creator of all that exists. Human beings, made in God's image, share to some degree in the "likeness" of God, but are as distinct from God as earthly children are from their parents. God is our source and our destiny; and the only way to know our own true identity and follow the one true path to salvation, is to "listen" to God and "obey." Seeking is more important as an attitude than an activity. It means not that we are looking for the lost God, but that we are aware that unless God speaks to us and leads us, we are lost. Seeking is not aimed primarily at finding a system of rules and principles, but in finding a relationship with our Maker who declares boldly that we are the objects of divine love. God loves all peoples of the earth, but has chosen to speak most directly and audibly to and through one small family clan consisting of the Middle-East pilgrim and patriarch Abram (Abraham) and his wife Sarai (Sarah). These faithful early "listeners" obeyed the voice of God and were therefore chosen as God's own contagious witnesses so that all humanity would eventually be blessed.

Now the LORD said to Abram, "Go from your country [present day Iraq] and your kindred and your father's house to the land that I will show you. I will make of you a great nation, and I will bless you, and make your name great, so that you will be a blessing. . . . So Abram went, as the LORD had told him. . . .

When Abram was ninety-nine years old, the LORD appeared to Abram, and said to him, "I am God Almighty; walk before me, and be blameless. And I will make my covenant between me and you, and will make you exceedingly numerous." Then Abram fell on his face; and God said to him, "As for me, this is my covenant with you: You shall be the ancestor of a multitude of nations. No longer shall your name be Abram, but your name shall be Abraham; for I have made you the ancestor of a multitude of nations. I will make you exceedingly fruitful; and I will make nations of you, and kings shall come from you. I will establish my covenant between me and you, and your offspring after you throughout their generations, for an everlasting covenant, to be God to you and to your offspring after you. (Genesis 12:1-2, 4; 17:1-7)

The unfolding story of God's design to speak to and bless all nations through the lineage of Abraham and Sarah is the rest of the Bible. In the generations that follow more children are born. Some heed the voice of God, some do not. Abraham and Sarah's miracle son, born in their old age, is named Isaac. Through his line the blessing is passed. His son Jacob, later named Israel, meaning "he who strives with God," is the father of twelve sons who multiply to become the twelve tribes of Israel. Israel's youngest son, Joseph, carries the witness to Egypt; and even the Pharaoh recognizes a unique manifestation of God in Joseph and declares:

Pharaoh said to his servants, "Can we find anyone else like this—one in whom is the spirit of God?" So Pharaoh said to Joseph, "Since God has shown you all this, there is no one so discerning and wise as you. You shall be over my house, and all my people shall order themselves as you command; only with regard to the throne will I be greater than you." (Genesis 41:38-40)

But the extension of the contagious witness and obedience to the voice of God did not continue uninterrupted. It never has. The Bible asserts that from the creation of our earliest ancestors, human beings often choose to exercise their independent wills—a mark of God necessary for us to be made in the divine image—in rebellion

20

against God's will. God speaks, but we do not always listen, or at least we choose not to obey the voice of God. The story continues:

Now a new king arose over Egypt, who did not know Joseph. He said to his people, "Look, the Israelite people are more numerous and more powerful than we. Come, let us deal shrewdly with them...." The Egyptians became ruthless in imposing tasks on the Israelites, and made their lives bitter with hard service in mortar and brick and in every kind of field labor.

God heard their groaning, and God remembered his covenant with Abraham, Isaac, and Jacob.

Moses was keeping the flock of his father-in-law Jethro.... God called to him out of the bush, "Moses, Moses!" And he said, "Here I am."... Then the LORD said, "I have observed the misery of my people who are in Egypt; I have heard their cry on account of their taskmasters. Indeed, I know their sufferings, and I have come down to deliver them.... So come, I will send you to Pharaoh to bring my people, the Israelites, out of Egypt. But Moses said to God, "Who am I that I should go to Pharaoh, and bring the Israelites out of Egypt?" He said, "I will be with you. (Exodus 1:8-10, 13-14, 24; 3:1, 4, 7-8, 10-12)

God's design as revealed in the pages of the Bible is to set the captives free, and to make a covenant with all who know him as Savior and Redeemer, saying:

Do not fear, for I am with you;
    I will bring your offspring from the east,
    and from the west I will gather you;
I will say to the north, "Give them up,"
    and to the south, "Do not withhold;
bring my sons from far away
    and my daughters from the end of the earth—
everyone who is called by my name,
    whom I created for my glory,
    whom I formed and made."
Bring forth the people who are blind, yet have eyes,
    who are deaf, yet have ears!
Let all the nations gather together,
    and let the peoples assemble.
Who among them declared this,
    and foretold to us the former things?
Let them bring their witnesses to justify them,
    and let them hear and say, "It is true."

21

You are my witnesses, says the LORD,
   and my servant whom I have chosen,
so that you may know and believe me
   and understand that I am he.
Before me no god was formed,
   nor shall there be any after me.
I, I am the LORD,
   and besides me there is no savior.
I declared and saved and proclaimed,
   when there was no strange god among you;
   and you are my witnesses, says the LORD. (Isaiah 43:5-12)

The God of the Bible speaks and acts in history, and has a purpose, a design, a love, and a destiny for all humanity, and even all creation. The God of the Bible is the one who "proclaims," the one who "saves," and the one who creates by covenant a special people to be servants of and witnesses to the divine plan in order to bring glory to God. Found within the covenant is a code to live by, a morality, an ethic. But the commandments are not given only to regulate human activities and keep peace. They are primarily a manifestation of God's own nature, and a means by which the witness of God's covenant people might become more contagious. God's covenant people are to be a "priestly kingdom and a holy nation" (Exodus 19:6) in order that the earth might "be filled with the knowledge of the glory of the Lord, as the waters cover the sea" (Habakkuk 2:14).

In fact, the main theme of the biblical story is that humankind has been created to reveal the glory of God by enjoying the divine presence and manifesting the divine character: holiness, righteousness, justice, mercy, truth, compassion, long-suffering, and above all, steadfast love. However, the Lord declares:

I reared children and brought them up, but they have rebelled against me. The ox knows its owner, and the donkey its master's crib; but Israel does not know, my people do not understand.... The whole head is sick, and the whole heart faint. From the sole of the foot even to the head, there is no soundness in it. (Isaiah 1:2-3, 5-6)

But God does not abandon the plan. The purpose of creation will be accomplished. "The glory of the Lord shall be revealed, and all flesh shall see it together, for the mouth of the Lord has spoken" (Isaiah 40:5). There will be a new covenant.

The days are surely coming, says the LORD, when I will make a new covenant with the house of Israel and the house of Judah. It will not be like the covenant that I made with their ancestors when I took them by the hand to bring them out of the land of Egypt—a covenant that they broke, though I was their husband, says the LORD. But this is the covenant that I will make with the house of Israel after those days, says the LORD: I will put my law within them, and I will write it on their hearts; and I will be their God, and they shall be my people. No longer shall they teach one another, or say to each other, "Know the LORD," for they shall all know me, from the least of them to the greatest, says the LORD; for I will forgive their iniquity, and remember their sin no more. (Jeremiah 31:31-34)

There are other Old Testament descriptions of what the "new testament" or the new covenant will be like. But one other significant ingredient that begins to emerge is that what was begun through a family clan named after the faithful patriarch Abraham, will be completed through a new people created by God's own special ambassador, the true Servant, the Messiah, the Son of Man, the Son of God.

Thus when John the Baptist arrives on the scene, he sees his role in terms of announcing the arrival and preparing the way for the promised messianic age and the Messiah himself especially as depicted in Isaiah's prophecies. Mark begins his account of the gospel saying:

The beginning of the good news of Jesus Christ, the Son of God.
As it is written in the prophet Isaiah,
"See, I am sending my messenger ahead of you,
　who will prepare your way;
the voice of one crying out in the wilderness:
　'Prepare the way of the Lord,
　make his paths straight,' "
John the baptizer appeared in the wilderness, proclaiming a baptism of repentance for the forgiveness of sins....

He proclaimed, "The one who is more powerful than I is coming after me; I am not worthy to stoop down and untie the thong of his sandals. I have baptized you with water; but he will baptize you with the Holy Spirit." (Mark 1:1-4, 7-8)

When Jesus arrives, John declares "Here is the Lamb of God who takes away the sin of the world! This is he of whom I said, 'After me comes a man who ranks ahead of me because he was before me.... And I myself have seen and have testified that this is the Son of God' " (John 1:29, 34). Returning to Galilee Jesus begins his own ministry "proclaiming the good news of God, and saying 'The time is fulfilled, and the kingdom of God has come near, repent, and believe in the good news' " (Mark 1:14-15).

Later, in his hometown of Nazareth, as he enters the synagogue on the Sabbath he is offered the scroll of the prophet Isaiah to read. It must have seemed bothersome to many as he methodically unrolled the large scroll all the way to the back, intentionally selected a controversial messianic text and read:

"The Spirit of the Lord is upon me,
because he has anointed me
to bring good news to the poor.
He has sent me to proclaim release to the captives
and recovery of sight to the blind,
to let the oppressed go free,
to proclaim the year of the Lord's favor."
And he rolled up the scroll, gave it back to the attendant, and sat down. The eyes of all in the synagogue were fixed on him. Then he began to say to them, "Today this scripture has been fulfilled in your hearing." (Luke 4:18-21)

Later in the same conversation, Luke reports that all in the synagogue were filled with rage and drove Jesus from their town, with some wishing to kill him on the spot (Luke 4:28-29).

It is not possible for thoughtful people to calmly accept Jesus and his claims. They are far too radical. A multitude of books has been written to discover the "real Jesus" by those who even today find it impossible to think that any good Jewish man (which Jesus seemed to be) could have claimed the things for himself that are reported in the New Testament. No wonder he created a stir and even near riots everywhere he went if he truly announced through both his deeds and his words, though sometimes with ambiguous images and in muted tones, "I am God's messiah, come to inaugurate my Father's new covenant."

The Contagious God

Who or what is God? We can see something of God in creation, but we are dependent on a much more personal self-revelation if we

24

are to become personally acquainted with and live in harmony with God's purpose for us. There is considerable evidence that God has spoken to humanity, and the clearest, most consistent, voice of God is recorded in the Bible. In fact it is referred to as "God's Word."

In the earlier parts of the Bible referred to as the Hebrew Bible or the Old Testament, the voice of God comes primarily through prophets. These divine spokesmen were selected by God, often without regard for their personal preferences,[5] to reveal the divine will and interpret God's actions in history. "Thus says the Lord" was their frequent announcement of authority.

In the more recent part of the Bible known as the New Testament, Jesus claims to be more than a prophet. In fact he claims to be the fulfillment of the promises of God,[6] the embodiment of the voice of God,[7] and even the very presence of God, claiming "if you have seen me, you have seen the Father."[8] What's more, he claims to have set loose on the face of the earth a great contagion variously referred to as: "the kingdom of God," "the new covenant," or "eternal life." The nature of this "good infection" will be examined more closely in the next chapter, but first we have to face the problem Jesus creates by being more than we easily know how to handle.

The Jesus Problem

Is not God the one beyond us, "the high and lofty one who inhabits eternity?" (Isaiah 57:15). Is not God the one and only true God (Deuteronomy 6:4), who jealously guards and protects the divine identity and the divine name (Leviticus 20:1-7), and shares glory with no one (Isaiah 41:8)? Without question the Bible clearly emphasizes that God is the one and only true God who is protective of the kind of revelation allowed. Again and again God's true nature is clarified and contrasted with both the "idols" which are "no gods" and with mortals.

Has a nation changed its gods,
    even though they are no gods?
But my people have changed their glory
    for something that does not profit.
Be appalled, O heavens, at this,
    be shocked, be utterly desolate,
        says the LORD,

for my people have committed two evils:
   they have forsaken me,
the fountain of living water,
   and dug out cisterns for themselves,
cracked cisterns
   that can hold no water. (Jeremiah 2:11-13)

Because your heart is proud
   and you have said, "I am a god;
I sit in the seat of the gods,
   in the heart of the seas,"
yet you are but a mortal, and no god,
   though you compare your mind
with the mind of a god. (Ezekiel 28:2)

For my thoughts are not your thoughts,
   nor are your ways my ways, says the LORD.
For as the heavens are higher than the earth,
   so are my ways higher than your ways
and my thoughts than your thoughts. (Isaiah 55:8-9)

It is clear in the Bible that God is not a mortal, and mortals are not God. But what will we do with this one called Jesus Christ, who stretches the boundary between being God and being human to the point of breaking? Who is this Son of Man and Son of God?

These are not small questions and they deserve far more attention than is intended in this short section. The goal here is not to treat this topic exhaustively, but sketch the outline of the problem before looking at some of the solutions.

First, there is the problem of how to interpret some of Jesus' actions and claims of authority. For example, it was clear by the Old Testament that God alone was the final and supreme Judge of the inward attitudes and the outward actions of both individuals and nations. Who else could possibly be equipped with the necessary wisdom and justice required?[9] Yet, Jesus actively poses as one directly involved in this judgment, both here in the present world, and at the end of time. When he brings healing to a paralytic he also announces "Son, your sins are forgiven" (Mark 2:5). The scribes are stunned! They know that forgiveness of sins, especially in this larger sense, is something only God can do. It is part of the divine prerogative of judgment. How could any man presume to utter such words? But Jesus simply acknowledges that he, as the "Son of Man," has this authority. Likewise when he describes the final judgment he speaks of himself as the one dividing the sheep from the goats (Matthew 25:31-46), and elsewhere declares:

> Very truly, I tell you, the Son can do nothing on his own, but only what he sees the Father doing; for whatever the Father does, the Son does likewise.... The Father judges no one but has given all judgment to the Son, so that all may honor the Son just as they honor the Father. (John 5:19, 22-23)

The early church therefore announced as part of the gospel that Jesus, whom God had raised from the dead, had been appointed to judge the world in righteousness (Acts 10:42; 17:31; 24:25).[10] And later the church's early creeds included "he shall come to judge the quick and the dead."

Out of such claims it is not hard to see how another major theme, that of "salvation," emerges as part of the Jesus Problem. Of course, the name "Jesus" (not entirely an uncommon name in that day) means "he is savior." Jesus boldly claims this as his identity and his task.

> Indeed, just as the Father raises the dead and gives them life, so also the Son gives life to whomever he wishes.... Very truly, I tell you, anyone who hears my word and believes him who sent me has eternal life, and does not come under judgment, but has passed from death to life. "Very truly, I tell you, the hour is coming, and is now here, when the dead will hear the voice of the Son of God, and those who hear will live. For just as the Father has life in himself, so he has granted the Son also to have life in himself; and he has given him authority to execute judgment, because he is the Son of Man. (John 5:21, 24-27)

Following this lead the early church openly proclaimed that Jesus was the only Savior, and the Savior of the whole world.[11] Yet, it is both God who saves (2 Timothy 1:9) and Jesus who saves (1 Timothy 1:15; Revelation 7:9-10). God saves through Jesus.

> For God so loved the world that he gave his only Son, so that everyone who believes in him may not perish but may have eternal life. Indeed, God did not send the Son into the world to condemn the world, but in order that the world might be saved through him. (John 3:16-17)

Even if another explanation could be offered for these two blend-ings of divine action and human action in the life of Jesus, several additional affirmations about Jesus make it difficult to separate him from sharing in some unique way in the divine nature. As the one risen from the dead he is identified with divine wisdom, acknowl-edged as preexistent, and clearly said to have had a part in or been responsible for creation itself (John 1:1-3; 8:58; 1 Corinthians 1:24, 30; 8:6; 10:4; 2 Corinthians 8:9; Colossians 1:15-17; Hebrews 1:2-3; 1 John 1:1-3). He is seen as worthy of worship and receives doxolo-gies of glory and praise along with God the Father (Philippians 2:10-11; 2 Peter 3:18; 2 Timothy 4:18; Hebrews 13:20-21; Revelation 1:5-6; 5:11-14). He is declared to be the "Lord"[12] (John 20:28; Acts 2:36; Philippians 2:11) and prayers are addressed to him (Acts 7:59-60; 1 Corinthians 16:22; 2 Corinthians 12:8; Revelation 22:20). Although infrequent, and sometimes with debate about the best translation of the Greek text, Jesus is at times outright referred to as "God"[13] (John 1:1; 20:28; Hebrews 1:8; 1 John 5:20) and frequently as one sharing equal billing with God (John 17:3; 2 Thessalonians 1:12; James 1:1; 2 Peter 1:1). What is quite clear is that early on, although Jesus seems to have preferred the designation "Son of Man," the alterna-tive title "Son of God" became the norm. And with this title some-thing new was beginning to emerge as the heart of the "Jesus Problem." What was the nature of this special relationship between God the Father and Jesus the only begotten Son of God?

Four Options

Efforts to make sense of the unique claims of Jesus are myriad, but the most common fall into four main categories. First, some would say that Jesus was a prophet who did miracles and had much good to teach us; however, he was mistaken about his identity as the unique Son of God and Savior of the world. A second approach, similar to the first but much more cautious about the "supernatural" in general, would also accept Jesus as a prophet and teacher, but assign the problem of his mistaken identity to the overly enthusias-tic writers in the early church. Both of these solutions to the prob-lem assume there is a real problem about the identity claims attributed to Jesus in the New Testament, and acknowledge they are "mistakes."

The third approach resolves the problem by accepting the claims of Jesus and attributing to him a kind of divinity, as much as any mortal could have, but limiting him to something like a heavenly messenger, created by God, sent by God, empowered by God, but subordinate to God. One variation of this approach acknowledges that Jesus is unique, divine, and the Son of God; but as such, he is subordinate to God the Father who is the only true God. A second variation sometimes is sounded by those who wish to remind us that Jesus himself said we were all "gods" and that those who believed in him would do "even greater works" than he did.[14] This is similar to what many in the New Age movement emphasize. God is the heavenly Father of Jesus and is our heavenly Father too. Therefore, we are all divine "sons of God" or "children of God." Although persons choosing this third approach would perhaps come out in very different camps regarding human nature, they nevertheless solve the problem of Jesus' claims about sharing in the divine nature by subordinating him to God Almighty, the *one* true God.

The fourth approach also recognizes that the claims and actions of Jesus present a new problem challenging the revelation of God found in the Old Testament. But as the church worked on this problem in light of Christian experience and the New Testament record, they found the best solution was to accept that Jesus brought a new level or new dimension of God's self-revelation, and they chose to describe this greater revelation as the Holy Trinity—Father, Son, and Holy Spirit. The concept has confused many and stretched even the best theologians throughout the history of the church. But grasping the reality of this revelation offers more than just a solution to a theological and Christological problem. The revelation of God as Holy Trinity is one of the most important and one of the most neglected areas of teaching related to evangelism. It is here that we must begin if we are to truly understand the contagious nature of God and the nature of our Christian witness as part of that contagion. Without this solution to the "Jesus Problem," we remain only marginally aware of all the gospel means for the salvation of the world, and in fact we may without knowing it be bearing false witness.

God as Holy Trinity

Although reference to God as the Holy Trinity has been classical, orthodox Christianity for almost the entire history of the church, it has never been easily explained nor readily appreciated by the vast majority of ordinary Christians. Often it simply has been declared from the "top down" as "truth" without seeming to be the kind of truth Jesus referred to when he said "know the truth, and the truth will make you free" (John 8:32). My own experience of this concept as a child growing up was that it ranked as an important formula to dust off and recite in creeds, baptisms, and benedictions; but other-wise, it remained nicely tucked away like a family secret not to be discussed.

Thomas Jefferson, although a Deist and not a Christian, probably struck a note that many Christians would unwittingly say "amen" to if they could honestly express their own thoughts on the matter. In a letter to Timothy Pickering he wrote the following concerning his views on the Trinity:

> When we shall have done away with the incomprehensible jargon of the Trinitarian arithmetic, that three are one, and one is three; when we shall have knocked down the artificial scaffolding, reared to mask from view the simple structure of Jesus; when, in short, we shall have unlearned everything which has been taught since his day, and got back to the pure and simple doctrines he inculcated, we shall then be truly and worthily his disciples.[15]

Is the doctrine nothing more than "artificial scaffolding" hindering our view? Some would still say so. But scaffolding is only a barrier for those who remain outside at ground level trying to peer through it instead of making use of the free ticket in their hands to enter the grandstands. From the elevated view inside, the scaffolding is a great blessing that allows a whole new experience of the drama played out below, and a chance to become much more acquainted with the main actors.

Working to clarify the relationship between the one true God, Jesus Christ the Son of God, and the Holy Spirit was a difficult task for the early church. The writers of the New Testament became increasingly aware of the importance of this relationship, even though they never officially used the expression "Trinity." The term itself was first suggested by the North African theologian, Ter-tullian of Carthage, over a hundred years after the completion of the New Testament. But as we have seen in briefly exploring the "Jesus Problem," the roots of the doctrine are found in both the teaching of Jesus and in the experience of the first-century church.[16] For example:

> "If you know me, you will know my Father also. From now on you do know him and have seen him." Philip said to him, "Lord, show us the Father, and we will be satisfied." Jesus said to him, "Have I been with you all this time, Philip, and you still do not know me? Whoever has seen me has seen the Father.... And I will ask the Father, and he will give you another Advocate, to be with you forever. This is the Spirit of truth, whom the world cannot receive, because it neither sees him nor knows him. You know him, because he abides with you, and he will be in you." (John 14:7-9, 16-17)

> We declare to you what was from the beginning, what we have heard, what we have seen with our eyes, what we have looked at and touched with our hands, concerning the word of life—this life was revealed, and we have seen it and testify to it, and declare to you the eternal life that was with the Father and was revealed to us—we declare to you what we have seen and heard so that you also may have fellowship with us; and truly our fellowship is with the Father and with his Son Jesus Christ.... By this we know that we abide in him and he in us, because he has given us of his Spirit. And we have seen and do testify that the Father has sent his Son as the Savior of the world. God abides in those who confess that Jesus is the Son of God, and they abide in God. (1 John 1:1-3; 4:13-15)

The Holy Spirit is the Spirit of God the Father (Matthew 3:16; 10:20), the Spirit of Christ Jesus the Son (Galatians 4:6; Philippians 1:19), the Spirit of the Lord (Luke 4:18; Acts 5:9; 8:39), and occasionally several descriptions are used almost simultaneously, as in this passage from Romans 8:9-11.

> But you are not in the flesh; you are in the Spirit, since the Spirit of God dwells in you. Anyone who does not have the Spirit of Christ does not belong to him. But if Christ is in you, though the body is dead because of sin, the Spirit is life because of righteousness. If the Spirit of him who raised Jesus from the dead dwells in you, he who raised Christ from the dead will give life to your mortal bodies also through his Spirit that dwells in you.

The Father, the Son, and the Spirit are three, yet obviously in many ways one. How can this be best explained?

31

Through the ages many have attempted to de-mystify the divine "Trinity." Tertullian, the originator of the term, offered analogies such as "Root-Shoot-and-Fruit," "Spring-River-and-Channel," and "Sun-Beam-and-Point of Light" to explain the Father-Son-and-Holy Spirit relationship. This is actually quite helpful since a dynamic relationship is suggested rather than a static one (three sides of a triangle or three states of matter "solid-liquid-gas"). The problem with most trinitarian analogies, however, is they are non-personal. The relationship revealed in the Bible and in the experience of Christians through the ages is dynamic and deeply personal, i.e., related to three "persons" not just three aspects of time, space, and matter.

The most helpful contributions to make sense of the dynamic and yet personal and relational unity of God as Holy Trinity come from three theologians who lived and wrote in vastly different ages and contexts: Saint Augustine of North Africa (A.D. 354–430), Jonathan Edwards of New England (A.D. 1703–58), and C. S. Lewis of England (1898–1963). The unique thread holding these men and their ideas together is the understanding that God's essential nature is "Love" (1 John 4:8, 16).

Augustine emphasized above all the unity of God. There is one God who possesses a single nature, a single deity, a single majesty, a single glory, a single will, and a single operation of that will. It could be said that though there are three "persons" in the Trinity, there is only one "personality." Because of this, Augustine could conceive of no activity in which only the Father or the Son or the Holy Spirit would be involved apart from the unity of the other two. His most helpful new idea was to explain this unity and diversity by drawing on our understanding of love. The Holy Trinity is Love between the Father (the Source of love and the Lover) and the Son (God's perfect self-image eternally emanating from the mind of the Father, and the Object of the divine love), with the Holy Spirit constituting the Love Bond itself between the Father and the Son.[17] This image of God as solitary thinker and lover became the standard rationale of the Trinity for most of the next fifteen hundred years.

Jonathan Edwards in his writings on the Trinity reflects the influence of Augustine, as can be seen in the following.

The Father is the Deity subsisting in the prime, unoriginated and most absolute manner. The Son is the Deity subsisting in act, or the divine essence generated by God's understanding, or having an Idea of himself and subsisting in that Idea. The Holy Ghost is the Deity subsisting in act, or the divine essence flowing out and breathed forth in God's infinite love and delight in himself.[18]

But notice how the static, solitary Thinker-Lover is expanded in Edwards' description of the "sacred energy" in this love bond.

> The Godhead being thus begotten by God's loving an Idea of himself and shewing forth in a distinct subsistence or person in that Idea, there proceeds a most pure act, and an infinitely holy and sacred energy arises between the Father and Son in mutually loving and delighting in each other.... The deity becomes all act, the divine essence itself flows out and is as it were breathed forth in love and joy. So that the Godhead therein stands forth in yet another manner of subsistence, and there proceeds the third person in the Trinity, the Holy Spirit, viz. the deity in act.[19]

The Holy Spirit is the love of "God is love." Yet, Edwards sets the love of the triune God in motion "flowing" in joy, and finds himself uncomfortable with the dominating idea being restricted to "self-love." He does not resolve his own discomfort, but he suggests that we consider the possibility of thinking of the divine Mystery as a "society or Family of the Three."[20] Augustine had tightly bound the love of God into a self-love in order to protect the unity of God's oneness. Edwards believed the theological tether needed some loosening (while still being careful not to untie the knot altogether and slip into tri-theism) in order to make God's love more directly related to God's action in human history.

Many nineteenth and twentieth century theologians have greatly expanded our appreciation of God's nature as Holy Trinity. But perhaps no more helpful contribution has been made related to God's nature as divine love than that by C. S. Lewis in his masterful description of our heritage and faith in *Mere Christianity*. Lewis clarifies first of all why at least two "persons" are important if "God is love."

> All sorts of people are fond of repeating the Christian statement that "God is love." But they seem not to notice that the words "God is love" have no real meaning unless God contains at least two Persons. Love is something that one person has for another person. If God was a single person, then before the world was made, He was not love. [Christians] believe that the living, dynamic activity of love has been going on in God for ever and has created everything else.

And that, by the way, is perhaps the most important difference between Christianity and all other religions: that in Christianity God is not a static thing—not even a person but a dynamic, pulsating activity, a life, almost a kind of drama. Almost, if you will not think me irreverent, a kind of dance. The union between the Father and the Son is such a live concrete thing that this union itself is also a Person.[21]

Lewis goes on to explain that the Spirit who is generated out of the eternal love between the Father and the Son is in fact similar to the "spirit" generated in any communal relationship among humans. We easily speak of the spirit of the winning team, or of the losing team, or of a happy marriage, or of a couple facing divorce. This is the spirit of the relationship itself, something other than and yet a unique combination of the persons involved. In other relationships the spirit does not actually become a "person," but in the divine dance of love, the Spirit is truly Person who is one with and yet other than the Father and the Son. Lewis then writes:

And now, what does it all matter? It matters more than anything else in the world. The whole dance, or drama, or pattern of this three-Personal life is to be played out in each one of us; or (putting it the other way round) each one of us has got to enter that pattern, take his place in that dance. Good things as well as bad, you know, are caught by a kind of infection. If you want to get warm you must stand near the fire: if you want to be wet you must get into the water. If you want joy, power, peace, eternal life, you must get close to, or even into, the thing that has them. If you are close to it, the spray will wet you: if you are not, you will remain dry.[22]

It should almost be clear now why we need to talk about the contagious God. To say "God is love" means God as Creative Source (Father) and God as Perfect Image (Son) powerfully love each other in such a way that a contagious Holy Spirit is generated. Out of this eternal union all that is has been created. The Spirit of this love relationship communicates this ultimate reality of unity in diversity into every atom and cell of created matter. We who are made in the image of God, are uniquely designed to catch this "good infection." The Life of this eternal Love has come from the Father, in the Son, and reaches out to catch us in the Spirit *if* we will get close to the fountain.

34

An Invitation to Dance

If we can begin to see the nature of God as dynamic love between the Persons of the Trinity, than much of the Bible takes on a whole new hue. The story is not just about a holy God who demands conformity to a code, nor is it about beliefs that are either right or wrong, true or false, which will determine where we spend eternity. There is more. In fact, the triune God of love we have been describing, made us to be participants in and bearers of this same eternal life and love. Although in the Old Testament there are only hints and shadows of God as a unity and diversity that we now know as the Holy Trinity, there is a consistent and unfolding revelation of the character of God and of humanity's created purpose. The creation is "good." The first description of something "not good" is that "man should be alone" (Genesis 2:18). Our "humanness" and the image of God in us is in part revealed in that the two should become one (Genesis 2:24). In our "maleness" and "femaleness" there is a designed unity in diversity that reflects the image and nature of God. This is not to say that there are specific human gender qualities to be attributed to God, but there is a "oneness" in our human "twoness" that is necessary for God's image to be "good."

This oneness is much more than mere sexuality. It has to do with a bond that is eternal in a "covenant" of love. The Old Testament issues of unfaithfulness to one's wife or husband are serious not just for social reasons, but because God is both like a parent and like a marriage partner to each of us. The prophet Jeremiah speaks God's word reminding us of these images saying:

> And I thought you would call me, My Father,
>   and would not turn from following me.
> Instead, as a faithless wife leaves her husband,
>   so you have been faithless to me, O house of Israel,
> says the LORD. (Jeremiah 3:19-20)[23]

To break the covenant bond of love is to go contrary to the very nature of God and God's image in us. It reveals that we really do not "know" God. Thus, Jesus describes the life we are to share, eternal life, in these words. "And this is life eternal, that they may know you, the only true God, and Jesus Christ whom you have sent (John 17:3). Eternal life is a quality of life shared in an intimate "knowing" of God.

In the single verse cited above from John 17 we catch the central theme of what John records as the prayer of Jesus for his disciples and for all the world. Notice how this "high priestly prayer," as it is usually called, captures the longing of Jesus and his Father for all humanity to share in what the Godhead has always enjoyed.

> I have made your name known to those whom you gave me from the world. They were yours, and you gave them to me, and they have kept your word.... But now I am coming to you, and I speak these things in the world so that they may have my joy made complete in themselves ... that they may all be one. As you, Father, are in me and I am in you, may they also be in us. (17:6, 13, 21)

The dynamic relationship of unity in diversity that is in the God-head, the life that is eternal as a powerful and joyful union of love, is meant to be in us. God the Son was sent by God the Father into the world to restore humanity to this divinely ordained life by initiating this good infection that draws us in to God's dance of love. And each and every one of us is invited to accept this embrace and join in the dance.

Jesus usually called this contagious, redemptive opportunity the "kingdom of God," "eternal life," or the "new covenant." Some will think it best to stay with this language when describing the essence of the Christian gospel, and in the next chapter these and other images will be examined more carefully. But in keeping with the wonderfully refreshing image used by C. S. Lewis in describing the "dynamic, pulsating activity" of the Holy Trinity as "a kind of dance,"[24] some of you, along with me, may find this kind of invitation creatively energizing. Sydney Carter did when he wrote his hymn, "Lord of the Dance":*

> I danced in the morning when the world was begun,
> and I danced in the moon and the stars and the sun,
> and I came down from heaven and I danced on earth.
> At Bethlehem I had my birth.
> Dance, then, wherever you may be;
> I am the Lord of the Dance, said he.
> And I'll lead you all wherever you may be,
> and I'll lead you all in the dance, said he.[25]

Can you see it? Can you hear the voice of God with the accent of a Galilean Jewish carpenter asking you by name to come to the party, to join in the dance? Maybe you heard this inviting voice long ago and already have been dancing for years. In that case, may this book help you discover how to be a more contagious Christian witness of God's love for all. But if you are still trying to figure out what in the world I am talking about, I hope you will read on. And if at some time in the next few days or weeks or years you hear that inviting voice more clearly, I hope you will know that even those of us who are lame and twisted can be wondrously restored and filled with a Spirit of grace for this dynamic, liberating dance that has been going on in the cosmos from before the foundation of the world.

Come, let's dance.

"The whole creation is on tiptoe to see the wonderful sight" (Romans 8:19 JBP).

CHAPTER TWO

The Good Infection

"Infection—an influence or impulse passing from one to another and affecting feeling or action."

—*Webster's Encyclopedic Unabridged Dictionary*
of the English Language

Infections are not normally associated with words like "good" but with invisible microbes, pain, disease, and even death. We would be quite familiar with a headline from the Centers for Disease Control warning people to take precautions against an outbreak of E. coli 0157, tuberculosis, or some other infectious disease. Of course, the fact that a warning was issued would not necessarily affect all people the same way. Some would heed it, some would ignore it. Nevertheless, everyone who read about or heard the announcement would realize it was intended to protect people from "catching" the mysterious enemy so destructive to the human body and what we call health.

In contrast, what response might be given to an announcement about an "infectious ease"? To be quite honest, probably most of us would not even be sure we understood the language. The words don't seem to go together. What is an "ease"? *Webster's Encyclopedic Unabridged Dictionary of the English Language* defines the noun "ease" as: "freedom from labor, pain, physical annoyance, concern, anxiety, difficulty, great effort, need, stiffness, constraint, or formality." More positively it describes "tranquil rest, comfort, a quiet state of mind, unaffectedness, a sense of relaxation and well being." If there were an infectious ease, wouldn't it be delightfully good news to announce? Absolutely!

Announcing the Good Infection

The good news about a contagious life of love springing forth from the divine nature through the Lord of the Dance was the closing image of the previous chapter. We focused mostly on how this good infection of Eternal-Life-Love was at work in the Holy Trinity, God as Father-Son-Holy Spirit. In this chapter the goal is to describe more thoroughly the good infection itself. Later we will look at how it is passed from one carrier to another and try to uncover how it is "caught."

What is this good infection sometimes labeled the gospel, or the message of salvation, or the way to eternal life? Regardless of the name given, the task at hand is to identify as much as possible the inner workings of this good infection and describe what it does to persons who catch it. There are two primary sources for information: first, the Good-infection Book, the Bible; and second, case studies of those who tell their own stories. Let's begin with the Book.

Describing the gospel is challenging. For one thing, it is multifaceted and multidimensional; and in our attempts to make it understandable to as many people as possible, we have at times reduced it to something far too simplistic and flat. There are secrets to God's designs that we may never know, and surely we will not know them this side of eternity. However, as we examine this contagious life form from different angles, we can begin to see a cohesive and yet simplified order to the whole that is both exciting and life changing. It is something like Jesus must have had in mind when he said "know the truth, and the truth will make you free" (John 8:32).

Three strains of the gospel have been chosen for examination here. They are the biblical themes of the glory of God, the kingdom of God, and the new covenant. Again, these are not the only faces of the gospel worthy of careful examination. Others have explored the unifying themes of shalom, eternal life, salvation, liberation, and Christian discipleship to name just few. But a careful look at these three strains of the good infection will help establish its cohesive unity while respecting its wonderful diversity.

The Glory of God

The concept of "glory" includes such attributes as splendor, brilliance, excellence, magnificence, praiseworthiness, and in the original Hebrew "weight." If something was "heavy" it meant it was "full" of importance, honor, and even wealth. Most often when describing the glory of God, the Hebrew writers were reminding their readers that God was awesome beyond anything imagined. Yet God had revealed something of this awesome glory through what was created and through self-revelations known as the "shekina" or "dwelling with us glory." This presence of God is often recorded in the Bible as a penetrating, brilliant light or fire. Moses first experienced this radiant presence of the Lord when the bush on Mount Horeb was aflame but not consumed (Exodus 3:1-5). Later, all of the liberated children of Israel saw the glory on Mount Sinai. "Then Moses went up on the mountain, and the cloud covered the mountain. . . . Now the appearance of the glory of the Lord was like a devouring fire on the top of the mountain in the sight of the people of Israel" (Exodus 24:15, 17).

But the glory of God is more than the presence of God as a localized brilliant light. The glory of God is something that is intended to "fill the earth" (Numbers 14:21; Psalm 72:18-19) "as the waters cover the sea" (Habakkuk 2:14). The glory of God is the beauty of God revealed in all creation, and intended ultimately to be seen in the children of God "whom I created for my glory" (Isaiah 43:7). This beauty of God is also the holiness of God, the perfect purpose of God, and the righteous character of God. In fact, God's glory is best seen as God's "personal presence," which is literally in Hebrew the "face(s)"of God[1] Notice how the familiar Aaronic benediction captures this sense of God's glory as a blessing of his personal presence intended for us.

> The LORD bless you and keep you;
> the LORD make his face [literally "faces"] to shine upon you, and be gracious to you;
> the LORD lift up his countenance [literally "faces"] upon you, and give you peace. (Numbers 6:24-26)

God's glory shines on us as a radiant, personal presence—God's face—to bring us peace.[2]

The glory of God filling the earth is ultimately connected to God's children, who are uniquely designed to hold and to spread the glory as bearers of the image of God. But this reality is by no means automatic, it is dependent upon God's redemptive and saving work for all who will "turn to him in their hearts." Notice how these threads come together in this song of the psalmist.

Let me hear what God the LORD will speak,
for he will speak peace to his people,
to his faithful, to those who turn to him in their hearts.
Surely his salvation is at hand for those who fear him,
that his glory may dwell in our land.

Steadfast love and faithfulness will meet;
righteousness and peace will kiss each other.
Faithfulness will spring up from the ground,
and righteousness will look down from the sky. (Psalm 85:8-11)

This is the design. However, throughout the Old Testament the consistent problem is that God's children refuse their part in revealing the glory of God. They glory in themselves, or their own creations, or in other gods.

I reared children and brought them up,
but they have rebelled against me.
The ox knows its owner,
and the donkey its master's crib;
but Israel does not know,
my people do not understand.
Ah, sinful nation,
people laden with iniquity,
offspring who do evil,
children who deal corruptly,
who have forsaken the LORD,
who have despised the Holy One of Israel,
who are utterly estranged! (Isaiah 1:2-4)

For Jerusalem has stumbled
and Judah has fallen,
because their speech and their deeds are against the LORD,
defying his glorious presence. (Isaiah 3:8)
The more they increased,
the more they sinned against me;
they changed their glory into shame. (Hosea 4:7)

But in the midst of such continuing failure, God announces that there will be a way.

A voice cries out:
"In the wilderness prepare the way of the LORD,

make straight in the desert a highway for our God.
Every valley shall be lifted up,
  and every mountain and hill be made low;
the uneven ground shall become level,
  and the rough places a plain.
Then the glory of the LORD shall be revealed,
  and all people shall see it together,
for the mouth of the LORD has spoken." (Isaiah 40:3-5)

God will provide. The glory of God shall be revealed, and all shall see it.

The expectation emerges of a messiah who will embody God's glory and rescue God's people. In him the long-awaited revealing of the glory of God will be seen and God's children will emerge from their darkness into the wonderful light intended for all nations.

For darkness shall cover the earth,
  and thick darkness the peoples;
but the LORD will arise upon you,
  and his glory will appear over you.
Nations shall come to your light,
  and kings to the brightness of your dawn. (Isaiah 60:2-3)

The sun shall no longer be
  your light by day,
nor for brightness shall the moon
  give light to you by night;
but the LORD will be your everlasting light,
  and your God will be your glory. (Isaiah 60:19)

I am coming to gather all nations and tongues; and they shall come and shall see my glory, and I will set a sign among them. From them I will send survivors to the nations . . . to the coastlands far away that have not heard of my fame or seen my glory; and they shall declare my glory among the nations. (Isaiah 66:18-19)

Into this long-anticipated promise steps Jesus son of Mary and Son of God, prompting John to declare as he begins his Gospel:

There was a man sent from God, whose name was John. He came as a witness to testify to the light, so that all might believe through him.

He himself was not the light, but he came to testify to the light. The
true light, which enlightens everyone, was coming into the world....
And the Word became flesh and lived among us, and we have seen
his glory, the glory as of a father's only son, full of grace and truth....
No one has ever seen God. It is God the only Son, who is close to
the Father's heart, who has made him known. (John 1:6-9, 14, 18)

The amazing thing about the good infection of the glory of God
is not merely that Jesus is the Messiah who reveals the glory, but
that he is also the Savior and Redeemer who provides the means
by which the glory will be spread to all nations and cover the earth.
Jesus reveals this larger understanding of his coming on behalf of
his Father's glory in his prayer, which we looked at earlier.

I ask not only on behalf of these, but also on behalf of those who
will believe in me through their word, that they may all be one. As
you, Father, are in me and I am in you, may they also be in us, so
that the world may believe that you have sent me. The glory that you
have given me I have given them, so that they may be one, as we
are one, I in them and you in me, that they may become completely one, so that the world may know that you have sent me and have
loved them even as you have loved me. (John 17:20-23)

The glory of God in Jesus Christ is related to the oneness he
shares with the Father. This oneness is a oneness of love intended
to be manifested in those who believe in Jesus because they have
seen his glory as the glory of God. The glory is not inherent in being
human, for "all have sinned and fall short of the glory of God"
(Romans 3:23). But by God's undeserved grace Jews and Gentiles
alike are called not to be objects of wrath like faulty clay pots good
for nothing but destruction, but "to make known the riches of his
glory (as) objects of mercy, which he has prepared beforehand for
glory" (Romans 9:23).

And how is this glory revealed in us? How is it that our faulty clay
can show forth the radiant glory of God? Paul cautions that none of
us should think that the glory is any of our own doing. It must all
be to the honor and glory of God.

For who sees anything different in you? What do you have that you
did not receive? And if you received it, why do you boast as if it were
not a gift? (1 Corinthians 4:7)

For it is the God who said, "Let light shine out of darkness," who has shone in our hearts to give the light of the knowledge of the glory of God in the face of Jesus Christ. But we have this treasure in clay jars, so that it may be made clear that this extraordinary power belongs to God and does not come from us. (2 Corinthians 4:6-7)

So, the mystery is made clear. Christ, who is the glory of God, died and rose again in order that the tarnished darkness of sin might be replaced by the radiant glory of God in those who confess their need to be cleansed and restored, and receive the true light of life Jesus Christ into their own lives. To believe in Christ is only the means by which we open the door and receive the life of Christ, the glory of God, into our own beings.

Paul summarizes his whole ministry for Christ's body, the church, in these words:

I became its servant according to God's commission that was given to me for you, to make the word of God fully known, the mystery that has been hidden throughout the ages and generations but has now been revealed to his saints. To them God chose to make known how great among the Gentiles are the riches of the glory of this mystery, which is Christ in you, the hope of glory. (Colossians 1:25-27)

The wondrous glory of God fills the earth as the contagious life of God in Jesus Christ penetrates and overcomes human darkness and is welcomed to dwell within us as the Spirit of God, the Spirit of Christ, the Spirit of truth and holiness. Once more Paul tries to summarize the gospel of this good infection.

For this reason I bow my knees before the Father, from whom every family in heaven and on earth takes its name. I pray that, according to the riches of his glory, he may grant that you may be strengthened in your inner being with power through his Spirit, and that Christ may dwell in your hearts through faith, as you are being rooted and grounded in love. I pray that you may have the power to comprehend, with all the saints, what is the breadth and length and height and depth, and to know the love of Christ that surpasses knowledge, so that you may be filled with all the fullness of God. (Ephesians 3:14-19)

To be "filled with all the fullness of God" is to manifest God's glory and reveal the good infection at work.

The Kingdom of God

A second description of the contagious "good infection" and the one seemingly preferred by Jesus himself, is the kingdom of God.

Those of us who live in countries where the ideas of a "kingdom" and a "king" seem foreign, may find it difficult at first to adjust to this language and imagery. We may think the concepts associated with kingdoms (kings, queens, princes, princesses, realms, reigns, thrones, and subjects) are outdated, unworkable, oppressive, or at best only the stuff of fairy tales. But our knowledge, our biases, and our ignorance all need to be set aside as we listen to the biblical description of that reality we pray for every time we say "thy kingdom come, thy will be done, on earth as it is in heaven."

The idea of God's kingdom emerges slowly in the Bible. Although other nations and peoples had kings, Israel was predominantly a collection of tribes led by clan patriarchs and/or a specially called prophet such as Moses or Joshua. The first mention of God having a kingdom comes in Exodus 19:6 when Moses, returning from Mount Sinai with a message for the Israelites, reports why God rescued them from slavery in Egypt. "Now therefore, if you obey my voice and keep my covenant, you shall be my treasured possession out of all the peoples. Indeed, the whole earth is mine, but you shall be for me a priestly kingdom and a holy nation." In all the rest of the first five books of the Bible known as the Pentateuch or the Torah, there is no other mention of God's kingdom.

Kingships and kingdoms which were so common in the surrounding nations were normally seen as contrary to the ideal of God as the active and present ruler of Israel. This danger that a human king over God's people would be tempted to act like other kings and usurp the rule of God, is seen for example in Gideon's refusal to be king after leading Israel in a successful defeat of the Midianites.

> Then the Israelites said to Gideon, "Rule over us, you and your son and your grandson also; for you have delivered us out of the hand of Midian." Gideon said to them, "I will not rule over you, and my son will not rule over you; the LORD will rule over you." (Judges 8:22-23)

In fact, here is only one positive mention of Israel being allowed to have a king that shows up in the whole Torah.

When you have come into the land that the LORD your God is giving you, and have taken possession of it and settled in it, and you say, "I will set a king over me, like all the nations that are around me," you may indeed set over you a king whom the LORD your God will choose. One of your own community you may set as king over you; you are not permitted to put a foreigner over you, who is not of your own community. Even so, he must not acquire many horses for himself, or return the people to Egypt in order to acquire more horses, since the LORD has said to you, "You must never return that way again." And he must not acquire many wives for himself, or else his heart will turn away; also silver and gold he must not acquire in great quantity for himself. When he has taken the throne of his kingdom, he shall have a copy of this law written for him in the presence of the levitical priests. It shall remain with him and he shall read in it all the days of his life, so that he may learn to fear the LORD his God, diligently observing all the words of this law and these statutes, neither exalting himself above other members of the community nor turning aside from the commandment, either to the right or to the left, so that he and his descendants may reign long over his kingdom in Israel. (Deuteronomy 17:14-20)

It is obvious that there are dangers inherent in having a king or being a king. Kings tend to forget the community and focus on their own aggrandizement. A foreign king would have no sense of the true and ultimate lordship of Yahweh who delivered Israel for his own special purpose. Kings are easily tempted to make expedient political choices and become entangled in the ways of the world, turning their hearts away from being humble servants of the most high God. Any true king of Israel must remain constantly attentive to God's word, observe it, humble himself both before God and others, and model meekness in majesty.[3] Not an easy calling. How many could be worthy? According to the Bible, not many. God granted Israel's petition to have their own king, but warned them through the aging Samuel that kings chosen from among men are almost always disappointments.[4] Nevertheless, in keeping with the requirements set forth in Deuteronomy 17, God chooses through Samuel, the tall, young, handsome, and humble Saul to be Israel's first king. It seemed to all an excellent choice.[5] But even the best of men almost always failed as faithful and effective kings of God's people. Saul succumbs to trusting in his own wisdom, to vanity, and to vindictive arrogance. David, the brave young warrior with a pure heart, is selected to succeed Saul as the second king. He is in many

46

ways a great king and a man of God, but he too ignores the law of God and believes as king that he deserves whatever he desires. In lust he takes another man's wife, and by force and cunning deceit has him murdered.[6] Only after being confronted by the prophet of God, Nathan, does David confess his sin, repent, and in humility return to God.[7] It was a costly lesson, and there were some others; but because of his humble spirit, David is restored by the Spirit of God to lead God's people as "a man after God's own heart."

As David nears the end of his life, Israel has successfully defended itself against all enemies and become established. David's son Solomon is chosen by God to succeed his father as the third king of Israel. David announces: "Of all my sons, for the Lord has given me many, he has chosen my son Solomon to sit upon the throne of the kingdom of the Lord over Israel" (1 Chronicles 28:5). Notice that it is the "kingdom of the Lord over Israel," not David's kingdom or Israel's kingdom. God promises David "I will establish his kingdom forever if he continues resolute in keeping my commandments and my ordinances, as he is today" (1 Chronicles 28:7). Thus David counsels both his "community" and his son Solomon:

> Now therefore in the sight of all Israel, the assembly of the Lord, and in the hearing of our God, observe and search out all the commandments of the Lord your God; that you may possess this good land, and leave it for an inheritance to your children after you forever.
>
> And you, my son Solomon, know the God of your father, and serve him with single mind and willing heart; for the Lord searches every mind, and understands every plan and thought. If you seek him, he will be found by you; but if you forsake him, he will abandon you forever. Take heed now, for the Lord has chosen you to build a house as the sanctuary; be strong, and act. (1 Chronicles 28:8-10)

King Solomon, like his father David, is a gifted and successful king. Israel expands under his leadership to experience its golden age. But Solomon fails to heed all of God's requirements (Deuteronomy 17). He accumulated massive wealth, trusted in his thousands of horses and chariots, married a multitude of foreign wives, followed after some of their gods, and "did what was evil in the sight of the Lord, and did not completely follow the Lord" (1 Kings 11:6).

> "Therefore the Lord said to Solomon, 'Since this has been your mind and you have not kept my covenant and my statutes that I have com-

manded you, I will surely tear the kingdom from you and give it to your servant. Yet for the sake of your father David I will not do it in your lifetime; I will tear it out of the hand of your son'." (1 Kings 11:11-12)

And so the kingdom designed to be forever, began to collapse.

It was understood that "the glorious splendor" of God's reign and kingdom were everlasting, as part of God's witness to all people,[8] but even the best of human kings fell into temptation and abused their power. The kingdom is divided and falls into ruin, and the prophets of God announce divine judgment and grace as two gifts calling the people and their kings to "return to the Lord." The hope of God's promise of an everlasting kingdom shifts to the shoulders of a messianic king, an unnamed child to be born from the line of and for the throne of David.

> For a child has been born for us,
> a son given to us;
> authority rests upon his shoulders;
> and he is named
> Wonderful Counselor, Mighty God,
> Everlasting Father, Prince of Peace.
> His authority shall grow continually,
> and there shall be endless peace
> for the throne of David and his kingdom.
> He will establish and uphold it
> with justice and with righteousness
> from this time onward and forevermore.
> The zeal of the LORD of hosts will do this. (Isaiah 9:6-7)

A second more dramatic image of the arrival of this heavenly king is found in the vision of Daniel which came to him in a dream.

> As I watched in the night visions,
> I saw one like a human being[9]
> coming with the clouds of heaven.
> And he came to the Ancient One[10]
> and was presented before him.
> To him was given dominion
> and glory and kingship,
> that all peoples, nations, and languages
> should serve him.

His dominion is an everlasting dominion
  that shall not pass away,
and his kingship is one
  that shall never be destroyed. (Daniel 7:13-14)

The stage is set.

Into this thousand-year longing for the everlasting kingdom steps Jesus, who is uniquely qualified to be anointed king. He manifests perfectly the qualities of power, justice, humility, simplicity, and total dependence on the will of God as established in Deuteronomy 17. He is of the royal lineage of David. Matthew's Gospel, written primarily for Jews, clearly has this in mind as it opens with "an account of the genealogy of Jesus the Messiah, the son of David" (Matthew 1:1). All the signs and songs of heaven announce his coming as the Gentile magi come from afar asking "Where is the child who has been born king of the Jews?" (Matthew 2:2); and the angel Gabriel counsels Mary "He will be great, and will be called the Son of the Most High, and the Lord God will give him the throne of his ancestor David. He will reign over the house of Jacob forever, and of his kingdom there will be no end" (Luke 1:32-33); and a full chorus of the heavenly host guide the shepherds to go see the birth of the Great Shepherd in the city of David (Luke 2:8-20).

The kingdom comes as the child king comes of age as a man. John the Baptist begins his ministry announcing "Repent, for the kingdom of heaven has come near" (Matthew 3:2); and Jesus echoes the identical message.

> From that time Jesus began to proclaim, "Repent, for the kingdom of heaven has come near." Jesus went throughout Galilee, teaching in their synagogues and proclaiming the good news of the kingdom and curing every disease and every sickness among the people. (Matthew 4:17, 23)[11]

The gospel of Jesus the Messiah *is* the gospel of the kingdom of God.

What Jesus announces he also demonstrates. The kingdom of God is the reign of God "on earth as it is in heaven." Jesus opens wide the doors of the kingdom to any who would "repent and believe." He heals the sick, restores sight to the blind, frees those in bondage to the demonic, forgives sinners, and teaches total reliance on God. The kingdom of God does not "abolish the law or the prophets" but "fulfills" them, deepens the meaning of them, and requires an even greater obedience and righteousness than the legalists of the day. The danger with any law is that it becomes an end in itself, a minimal, mechanical and self-justifying performance standard for legalists, and a wall raised against "outlaws" and "sinners" to the mercy of God. Jesus slices through both of these distortions of righteousness and justice and offers both groups the mercy and the power of God as he raises the standard to perfect love "so that you may be children of your Father in heaven" (Matthew 5:43-48).

When Jesus sends his twelve disciples out on their first missionary journey two by two he instructs them to "proclaim the good news, 'the kingdom of heaven has come near.' Cure the sick, raise the dead, cleanse the lepers, cast out demons" (Matthew 10:7-8). The kingdom of God[12] is not just good news as information, it is also the good news of transformation. It is a demonstration of God's active, loving, powerful, and present reign over the lives of those who submit to God the Father's authority through God the Son, Jesus the Messiah and King (Luke 19:37-40). It has a special concern for the poor and the downtrodden (Matthew 5:3; James 2:5). It is to be sought above all other things (Matthew 6:33). It is not merely a matter of saying "Lord, Lord" but it is about doing the Father's will (Matthew 7:21-23). It is worth losing everything else in order not to miss the kingdom (Matthew 13:44-46) for the rewards are multiplied both in this life and in the life to come (Luke 18:28-30). But one must enter it as a humble child with empty hands (Luke 18:17) and not like a person full of self and wealth (Luke 18:18-26). In fact, one must be "born again from above by the Spirit" to see the kingdom clearly and enter it (John 3:1-10). The kingdom is not merely something external to talk about coming in the future, it is already here among us and is intended to be within us (Luke 17:20-21).

Some have felt that the reason we hear so little about the kingdom of God today in evangelism is that after Jesus' death and resurrection the early church and the rest of the New Testament writers shifted to another emphasis. Although undoubtedly there were shifts in emphasis and dominant themes as the church grew and the gospel spread, such a blanket statement about the absence of the centrality of the kingdom is a mistake. Luke's second volume, Acts, begins with a reminder that the priority had not changed for the risen Jesus. "After his suffering he presented himself alive to them by many convincing proofs, appearing to them during forty days and speaking about the kingdom of God" (Acts 1:3). When questioned by his disciples, Jesus immediately instructs them that the one thing they need to know about the kingdom is that they must receive the gift of the Holy Spirit so that they will be able to extend the kingdom to "the ends of the earth" (Acts 1:4-8). The Apostle Paul in his travels "spoke out boldly, and argued persuasively about the kingdom of God" (Acts 19:8) and taught "about the Lord Jesus Christ with all boldness and without hindrance" (Acts 28:31). Likewise, instruction concerning the kingdom appears in eight of Paul's letters and epistles[13] as well as in Hebrews, James, 2 Peter, and John's Revelation.

How might the "gospel of the kingdom of God" best be summarized? Many scholars, preachers, and few evangelists have addressed this challenge, but there is something special about the efforts of E. Stanley Jones. In an age when almost no one was talking about the Kingdom of God, E. Stanley Jones missionary to India, world evangelist, celebrated author declared he was obsessed by the kingdom. It appears as the central theme in almost every book he wrote and helps us link the kingdom theme to what was learned about the glory of God and what will be seen about the nature of the new covenant. Jones writes:

> Jesus didn't define the Kingdom in precise terms, perhaps because he was the definition. We may define the Kingdom since he has shown us what it is—shown us in his own person, as: The Kingdom of God is God's total order, expressed as realm and reign, in the individual and in society; and which is to replace the present unworkable order with God's order in the individual and in society; and while the nature of the Kingdom is social, the entrance into it is by a personal new birth now; the character of the Kingdom is seen in the character of Jesus—the Kingdom is Christlikeness universalized.[14]

The kingdom of God is the reign of God activated throughout the entire human realm by the authority, power, and presence of the Son of God, Jesus Christ, transforming all relationships by the Holy Spirit into those that glorify God and manifest God's nature as perfect love. The kingdom of God is "righteousness and peace and joy in the Holy Spirit" (Romans 14:17) and not a matter of words but power (1 Corinthians 4:20). The kingdom is among us now, and will come in its final glory and fullness at the reappearing of the king

(Matthew 25:31-46). Then every knee shall bow and every tongue confess that "Jesus Christ is Lord, to the glory of God the Father" (Philippians 2:10).

Thy kingdom come! Thy will be done!

The New Covenant

One of the problems some Christian spokespersons have had with any number of the themes we are tracing is they neglect the inherent unity of the Bible. Some prefer to think that the Old Testament is "old" and therefore largely unworthy of Christian study. Without it, we have no idea of the primary meaning of Jesus as the "fulfillment." We fall into the spiritual game of "making it up as we go along." Our goal must be the same as that of Paul, who declared to the Ephesian elders, "I did not shrink from declaring to you the whole purpose of God" and counseled them to "keep watch over yourselves and over all the flock, of which the Holy Spirit has made you overseers" (Acts 20:27-28). Therefore, as we now seek to understand more of the "whole purpose of God" by examining the new "covenant" or "testament," we begin again with the old.

The idea of a covenant between God and the people of God is one of the most important concepts in the entire Bible. The expression appears almost three hundred times from Genesis 6:18 to Revelation 11:19. At its core a covenant is a sacred agreement of promise. It is a formalized relationship of mutual trust and responsibility with clarified expectations and benefits. Covenants between human agents assume the form of legal contracts. Oaths are taken in a public context, and in the earliest forms recorded in the Bible and in other literature of Middle Eastern antiquity, a covenant is "cut." Abraham, coming from Mesopotamia, would have been familiar with the tradition of "cutting" slaughtered animals in two when making (literally "cutting") a covenant. The significance is a very serious object lesson something like the childhood promise many of us remember "Cross my heart, hope to die, stick a needle in my eye." Both participants in the covenant walk back and forth between the divided halves of the sacrificed animals, promising "If I break this covenant, may this be my fate."[15] Cutting a covenant is a serious matter of truthfulness and faithfulness. It is a matter of life and death.

In the covenant God cuts with Abraham (Genesis 15), the animals are prepared; and as the sun is going down, Abraham falls into a deep sleep and a "terrifying darkness descended upon him" (15:12). God then promises Abraham that his offspring will have a land of their own, and that Abraham will go to his ancestors in peace at an old age. The interesting variable in the cutting of this covenant is that Abraham remains a passive participant sleeping through it, while a "flaming torch" representing God's presence "passed between the pieces" (15:17). God's covenants, unlike those between humans, rest entirely on divine initiative and execution. God takes ultimate responsibility, and though faithfulness is expected from Abraham, it is the grace of God and intimate communion that make it possible, not the iron-willed promise of Abraham. The final "cutting" of this covenant is in human flesh, male circumcision (Genesis 17:9-14), as an ever-present reminder of God's presence and promise that "I will establish my covenant" (17:19).

The time arrives for the offspring of Abraham to inherit the promised land. God appears to Moses in a burning bush and sends him to Egypt to lead the children out of slavery and into a land flowing with milk and honey. The exodus is accomplished. God intervenes with a multitude of signs and wonders. The liberated slaves seem to have every reason to trust in their Deliverer, but in the wilderness they quickly forget the blessings of yesterday and become a company of complainers. Step after tired step, month after month, they alternate between promises of enthusiastic faithfulness to God and fickle, quarreling disobedience. The dance seems to be two steps forward and two steps back. Finally, the covenant relationship is clarified as God "cuts" the ten commandments into stone and Moses delivers the tablets to the people who have promised "Everything that the Lord has spoken we will do" (Exodus 19:8). The face of Moses shines with the glory of God as he returns from his encounter with the Lord on the mountain. It is only a temporary radiance, however, quickly fading; but it serves as foreshadowing of Israel's own quickly fading faithfulness to God's covenant of "the law."

Although the form of making covenant changes through the centuries, each new version is a reminder that God's purpose is "an awesome thing that I will do with you" (Exodus 34:10). God will provide peace and blessing for the people and they will be "a priestly kingdom and a holy nation" (Exodus 19:6) for the glory of God. But the danger is clear from the beginning.

When the LORD your God has brought you into the land that he
swore to your ancestors, to Abraham, to Isaac, and to Jacob ... take
care that you do not forget the LORD, who brought you out of the
land of Egypt, out of the house of slavery. (Deuteronomy 6:10, 12)

Indeed, God's love is long-suffering and full of grace. But
whether the covenant is cut in flesh or in stone, it never seems to
cut deeply into the hearts of God's people; and the consequences
are far more devastating than anyone would be willing to acknowledge. We often think "spiritual" things are only that, something
added to the "real" world we face day after day. But the covenant
God of the Bible announces that neglecting holiness[16] and selecting
sin brings an ever-widening path of destruction and death instead
of the promised blessing.

> The earth dries up and withers,
>   the world languishes and withers;
>   the heavens languish together with the earth.
> The earth lies polluted
>   under its inhabitants;
> for they have transgressed laws,
>   violated the statutes,
>   broken the everlasting covenant.
> Therefore a curse devours the earth,
>   and its inhabitants suffer for their guilt;
> therefore the inhabitants of the earth dwindled,
>   and few people are left. (Isaiah 24:4-6)

The Lord calls prophets to be covenant messengers declaring
both judgment and hope. Isaiah announces:

> Therefore hear the word of the LORD, you scoffers
> who rule this people in Jerusalem.
> Because you have said, "We have made a covenant with death, ...
> for we have made lies our refuge,
> and in falsehood we have taken shelter";
> therefore thus says the Lord GOD,
> See, I am laying in Zion a foundation stone,
> a tested stone,
> a precious cornerstone, a sure foundation:
> "One who trusts will not panic."
> And I will make justice the line,

and righteousness the plummet;
hail will sweep away the refuge of lies,
and waters will overwhelm the shelter.
Then your covenant with death will be annulled. (Isaiah 28:14-18)

Here is my servant, whom I uphold,
my chosen, in whom my soul delights;
I have put my spirit upon him;
he will bring forth justice to the nations. . . .
I am the LORD, I have called you in righteousness,
I have taken you by the hand and kept you;
I have given you as a covenant to the people,
a light to the nations, . . .
See, the former things have come to pass,
and new things I now declare;
before they spring forth,
I tell you of them. (Isaiah 42:1, 6, 9)

Jesus is the new "cornerstone" (Matthew 21:3-46; Acts 4:11), the new solid foundation (Luke 6:46-49; Ephesians 2:20), and the servant who brings forth the new thing, a new covenant.

The prophet Ezekiel clarifies even more precisely the nature of the new thing God will do.

Therefore say to the house of Israel, Thus says the Lord GOD: It is not for your sake, O house of Israel, that I am about to act, but for the sake of my holy name, which you have profaned among the nations to which you came. I will sanctify my great name, which has been profaned among the nations, and which you have profaned among them; and the nations shall know that I am the LORD, says the Lord GOD, when through you I display my holiness before their eyes. I will take you from the nations, and gather you from all the countries, and bring you into your own land. I will sprinkle clean water upon you, and you shall be clean from all your uncleannesses, and from all your idols I will cleanse you. A new heart I will give you, and a new spirit I will put within you; and I will remove from your body the heart of stone and give you a heart of flesh. I will put my spirit within you, and make you follow my statutes and be careful to observe my ordinances. (Ezekiel 36:22-27)

And Jeremiah's "new covenant" coincides very closely with Ezekiel's description.

The days are surely coming, says the LORD, when I will make a new covenant with the house of Israel and the house of Judah. It will not be like the covenant that I made with their ancestors when I took them by the hand to bring them out of the land of Egypt—a covenant that they broke, though I was their husband, says the LORD. But this is the covenant that I will make with the house of Israel after those days, says the LORD: I will put my law within them, and I will write it on their hearts; and I will be their God, and they shall be my people. No longer shall they teach one another, or say to each other, "Know the LORD," for they shall all know me, from the least of them to the greatest, says the LORD; for I will forgive their iniquity, and remember their sin no more. (Jeremiah 31:31-34)

The new covenant will consist of: (1) radical forgiveness, (2) intimate knowledge of the Lord, (3) God's law written on human hearts, and (4) being the people of God. It will involve a new outpouring and indwelling of God's Spirit (Ezekiel 36:27; Joel 2:28-29) for all, and will finally extend God's witness and light and blessings to all nations.

How does this list of prophecy compare with the message of the New Testament? First, there is radical forgiveness. As we saw in Chapter One, Jesus opened the flood gates to sinners by announcing forgiveness. He declared that his death, his body broken and his blood shed, was a means by which new covenant forgiveness of sins would be "poured out for many" (Matthew 26:28; Luke 22:20). He sends his disciples to forgive (John 20:23) and calls Paul to be his ambassador to the Gentiles and "open their eyes so that they may turn from darkness to light and from the power of Satan to God, so that they may receive forgiveness of sins and a place among those who are sanctified by faith in me" (Acts 26:18). Peter, on the day of Pentecost, instructs those who hear his first sermon and ask "What should we do?" to "Repent, and be baptized ... so that your sins may be forgiven" (Acts 2:38). And it is a total forgiveness including "no condemnation for those who are in Christ Jesus" (Romans 8:1) and God's promise fulfilled that "I will remember their sins ... no more" (Hebrews 10:15-18).[17] Absolute forgiveness offered to every truly penitent soul is the opening chorus of the new covenant. But it is only the beginning. There is more, much more.

Second, the new covenant provides for every participant the experience of "knowing God." The promise offered through Jeremiah was "they all shall know me, from the least of them to the greatest." In the old covenant only a few could claim to know God through direct encounter. Most of the people only knew information shared with them about God and that God was essentially unapproachable. The heart of the new covenant is this new intimacy with God, which Jesus describes as the essence of eternal life (John 17:3). Knowing the Father is related to knowing the Son. Jesus reminded many of the religious leaders of his day that they did not know God, which was why they did not recognize him.

> "You say, 'He is our God,' though you do not know him. But I know him . . . and I keep his word. Your ancestor Abraham rejoiced that he would see my day; he saw it and was glad." Then the Jews said to him, "You are not yet fifty years old, and have you seen Abraham?" Jesus said to them, "Very truly, I tell you, before Abraham was, I am." (John 8:54-59)

> Jesus said to him, "I am the way, and the truth, and the life. No one comes to the Father except through me. If you know me, you will know my Father also. . . . If you love me, you will keep my commandments. And I will ask the Father, and he will give you another Advocate, to be with you forever. This is the Spirit of truth, whom the world cannot receive, because it neither sees him nor knows him. You know him, because he abides with you, and he will be in you." (John 14:6, 7, 15-17)

Knowing God the Father is related to knowing the Son and knowing the Spirit. Paul reminds us that it is the Spirit who dwells within us who helps us to know our new relationship with God as children adopted by our "Abba, Father" (Romans 8:15). In the entire Old Testament God is referred to as "Father" only a few times, and usually in a more formal sense. But in the New Testament Jesus uses the expression nearly two hundred times, on occasion employing the Aramaic word "Abba," the intimate household form of the word Father, more like "Daddy" or "Papa." This gift of God's eternal love "poured into our hearts through the Holy Spirit" (Romans 5:5) is available to all, through Christ. But "whoever says, 'I have come to know him,' but does not obey his commandments, is a liar, and in such a person the truth does not exist" (1 John 2:4). To know him is to know full forgiveness and tender love; to love him and say we know him is to "walk as he walked" (1 John 2:6).

Third, the new covenant insures that God's law will be written on our hearts, not just on tablets of stone or on paper. Many mistakenly believe that the old covenant was about law and the new covenant is about grace. There is grace and law in both. Paul reminds us that "by grace you have been saved through faith, and this is not your own doing; it is the gift of God not the result of works, so that no one may boast." He goes on then immediately to say that God has created us as new creatures in Christ "for good works, which God prepared beforehand to be our way of life" (Ephesians 2:8-10). We don't do "good works" to be saved, but we are saved in order that we might do "good works" and glorify God, not ourselves. Human nature without the power of the Holy Spirit[18] cannot and indeed does not want to keep the law of God. In fact, to focus on achieving a right relationship with God[19] through our own efforts at obedience, leads only to frustration, condemnation, and "death"; but "to set the mind on the Spirit is life and peace" (Romans 8:6). The new covenant is not about a legal code that "kills" but about a Spirit who gives life (2 Corinthians 3:6).

> You show that you are a letter of Christ, prepared by us, written not with ink but with the Spirit of the living God, not on tablets of stone but on tablets of human hearts.
>
> Such is the confidence that we have through Christ toward God. Not that we are competent of ourselves to claim anything as coming from us; our competence is from God, who has made us competent to be ministers of a new covenant.... Now the Lord is the Spirit, and where the Spirit of the Lord is, there is freedom. And all of us, with unveiled faces, seeing the glory of the Lord as though reflected in a mirror, are being transformed into the same image from one degree of glory to another; for this comes from the Lord, the Spirit. (2 Corinthians 3:3-6, 17-18)

In the new covenant, God has provided through the Holy Spirit the resources needed to become like Christ, joyfully obedient to the Father's will, keeping the commandments, revealing from one degree of glory to another the fruit of the Spirit in our lives: "love, joy, peace, patience, kindness, generosity, faithfulness, gentleness, and self control" (Galatians 5:22). God's law is being written on our hearts.

Fourth, the new covenant is about being the new "people of God," not just new "persons of God." The new covenant is designed to manifest how in diversity we can be united in one Spirit. "There is no longer Jew or Greek, there is no longer slave or free, there is no longer male and female; for all of you are one in Christ Jesus" (Galatians 3:28). Christianity, as we sometimes call the formal structure of this new covenant, is not a private religion, but a corporate, reconciling, fellowship of brothers and sisters in the household of God. It is about young and old, women and men, poor and rich, Jews and Gentiles, persons from all languages, nations, and cultures united into one new body, the body of Christ. This is the revelation the world is waiting for as proof that this gospel is truly of God. Breaking down the inherited, cultural, ethnic, boundaries and "walls" that divide us (Ephesians 2:14-22) makes little sense to those of the "flesh" (human nature without the Spirit of God), but in Christ we are new creatures.

> From now on, therefore, we regard no one from a human point of view;[20] even though we once knew Christ from a human point of view, we know him no longer in that way. So if anyone is in Christ, there is a new creation: everything old has passed away; see, everything has become new! All this is from God, who reconciled us to himself through Christ, and has given us the ministry of reconciliation. (2 Corinthians 5:16-18)

Thus, the earliest members of this new body were drawn together on the day of Pentecost from "every nation under heaven" and the Spirit spoke in a multitude of languages to make one new covenant community "in the name of Jesus Christ" (Acts 2:1-39).

> They devoted themselves to the apostles' teaching and fellowship, to the breaking of bread and the prayers.... All who believed were together and had all things in common; they would sell their possessions and goods and distribute the proceeds to all, as any had need. Day by day, as they spent much time together in the temple, they broke bread at home and ate their food with glad and generous hearts, praising God and having the goodwill of all the people. And day by day the Lord added to their number those who were being saved. (Acts 2:42, 44-47)

And they were admonished to "consider how to provoke one another to love and good deeds, not neglecting to meet together, as is the habit of some, but encouraging one another" (Hebrews 10:24-25). The new covenant is a "one another" covenant with the "One for others" God who chose Abraham so that "all the families of the earth" would be blessed (Genesis 12:3) and sent Jesus "that the world might be saved through him" (John 3:17).

Identifying Common Strains

One of the tasks of diagnosing an infectious disease is recognizing which symptoms are common to many related diseases and which are unique to the particular infection contracted. My teenage son was having problems with a sore throat, a low-grade fever, and swollen tonsils—good signs of an infection. A trip to the doctor was in order. After examining the patient and running a quick test for the streptococcus bacteria (which was negative), the doctor said "Well, this could be lots of things, but if he were my son I'd give him some antibiotics just in case." We filled the prescription and began to pump him full of the "good stuff." A week later the pain was still present and the tonsils were huge. We also noticed two or three tender and swollen lymph nodes on the back of his head and in his neck. Obviously the antibiotics had had little effect.

We were planning a family trip out of town for the next week during school break, so it was back to see the doctor. "It may be some sort of allergy," he said. "Let's just keep him on the antibiotics and when you get back call me if he's not better. I'll give him something for the pain."

Off we went on vacation only to notice after attending worship on Easter Sunday that a rash was emerging all over his face, neck, arms, hands, and trunk. His throat was still very sore, but he seemed to have little fever. This was frightening. We had been to the doctor! What was the problem? Was this strep, scarlet fever, or what? No place to go but to the emergency room at the closest hospital. After lots of forms were filled out and questions were asked, blood was drawn. The strep test came back negative, once more. More blood was drawn. Another lab test was run. Two and a half hours after arriving at the hospital we had an answer. It was mononucleosis. The antibiotic prescribed and taken faithfully actually contributed to worsening the symptoms and created the rash. Observing symptoms and treating them is not always helpful. The "real thing" may be masked by symptomatic features shared with other infections. It is critical to observe all of the symptoms in order to diagnose the actual condition of the patient. Otherwise, even the best-intended efforts to bring relief may in fact only make things worse.

Religion is a lot like the story above. There are actually many different "infections"; and although they may look alike, even to some "experts," they produce quite different results if allowed to run their full course. Being "religious" is not the same as being "alive in Christ." Even being "Christian" is not the same as being "alive in Christ." The good infection we have been describing must not be allowed to be lumped into the wrong category with other "look-alikes." Yes, many religions and even various outward manifestations of Christianity share much in common. But the "good infection" of the gospel of Jesus Christ is unique unto itself and must not be confused with "religious infections" in general. In fact, it is the opinion of this author that some have almost become immune to the "real infection" of God's forgiving and transforming presence and power in Jesus Christ, because they have been inoculated by various "doctors" and "doctrines" that only vaguely resemble the "the word of truth, the gospel" (Colossians 1:5). This has always been a problem for those seeking to pass on the authentic message of Christianity. "You foolish Galatians! Who has bewitched you?" wrote Paul (Galatians 3:1). And John warned, "We know that the Son of God has come and has given us understanding so that we may know him who is true; and we are in him who is true, in his Son Jesus Christ. He is the true God and eternal life. Little children, keep yourselves from idols" (1 John 5:20-21).

So what are the essential characteristics of the good infection? It should be clear by now that although there are different themes and strains of the gospel, each essentially tells the same story and announces the same fulfillment. Whether we trace the story of "glory," or the theme of the "kingdom," or the "covenant" strain, the central message is the same.

First, God is, by nature, Life and Love.

Second, God desires this Love-Life to be manifested in the world through human beings who are made in God's image.

Third, because human beings have misused God's gift of "freedom" so necessary for love, and distorted God's image by both personal and corporate sin, we all stand in need of being delivered from the deadly and destructive power of sin's disease before we can become "eased" and alive in Love through God's good infection.

Fourth, God's true and perfect reflection, the second person of the Trinity, Jesus Christ, came among us to display the glory of this Love-

Life in human form, and offer the only effective remedy to heal us from sin's "anti-glory" and restore in us God's glorious Love-Life.

Fifth, the divine remedy required a threefold intervention on our behalf. God the Holy Trinity: (1) absorbed the destructive force of our sin through Jesus' death on the cross; (2) demonstrated that this Jesus was God's true Son in the flesh by raising him from the dead to reveal that God had power over sin and death; and (3) established the new "good infection" community through the outpouring and indwelling of the Holy Spirit.

Sixth, this glorious contagion is freely available to all, but only becomes active in those who open themselves to it through faith in Christ who offers a divine cleansing and a regeneration of the full divine image in us through the indwelling Spirit.[21]

Seventh, this "salvation-healing" creates a contagious and glorious covenant-community known as the church, the body of Christ, the people of God, in order that directed and empowered by the Holy Spirit, they will spread the gospel of this good infection and fill the earth with the glory of God seen as "Christlikeness universalized."

Note from a Doctor

At various times in my life I have settled for less than the whole infection described above. Sometimes I did this because I didn't know the difference. I was ignorant. Ignorance in matters pertaining to both good and bad infections can be extremely dangerous. We need guides, teachers, and doctors who know the difference and have the God-given knowledge and wisdom to direct us as we move from the early stages of recovery from the destructive disease, into the ever-unfolding glory of being "participants of the divine nature" (2 Peter 1:4) and manifestations of the life "God has prepared for those who love him" (2 Corinthians 2:9).

One who made very effective use of the image of the gospel as God's ultimate medicine for both our temporal and eternal health (although not directly the image of a good infection), was the eighteenth-century English evangelist-reformer John Wesley. Everyone in his day did not agree with the imagery. Many felt he went too far with his positive attitude toward the human potential. But in reality, he saw little human potential apart from the redemptive intervention of God. England was a moral shambles, a society ready to implode on itself and only a step away from a bloody revolution akin to that which had shaken France half a century earlier. The church and religion were largely a formal toy of the aristocracy. Some sought to be serious about their faith, and practiced their piety in order that they might gain heaven, but few expected much from God in this life either for themselves or the masses.

Wesley himself spent thirty-five years of his life trying to find the "inward religion" that transformed shattered souls into the saints of God. All of his efforts only led him to despair. Then a band of lively and contagious Moravian missionaries convinced him that a form of contemporary Christianity existed like that of the primitive church. They spoke of the inward witness of the Spirit assuring all true believers in Christ that their sins were forgiven, that God loved them with a perfect love, and that this love was the true and perfect medicine of life intended for all humanity. Two more years passed before the reality of this "true religion" penetrated the mind and heart of John Wesley and began to shape him into one of England's most successful but least appreciated reformers.

His life-changing experience on May 24, 1738, at a small group meeting in London is recorded in his journal quite simply as follows:

> In the evening I went quite unwillingly to a society in Aldersgate Street where one was reading Luther's Preface to the Epistle to the Romans. And about a quarter before nine, while he was describing the change which God works in the heart through faith in Christ, I felt my heart strangely warmed. I felt I did trust in Christ, Christ alone for salvation: And an assurance was given me that he had taken away *my* sins, even *mine* and saved *me* from the law of sin and death.[22]

In the years that followed, John Wesley, his brother Charles, and several other friends who likewise discovered the transforming power of God that could work a "new birth" even in stubborn, grown men, shared this good news openly wherever any would listen. Some heard the news gladly, were awakened in their souls, and by faith began the journey of joy and salvation from "one degree of glory to another." Others, especially other clergy in the Church of England, resisted the message and the messengers, sometimes accusing both to be of the devil.

In *An Earnest Appeal to Men of Reason and Religion,* published in 1743, he set forth a defense of both what they taught and what was caught. He begins with a description of the need.

We see—and who does not?—the numberless follies and miseries of our fellow creatures. We see on every side either men of no religion at all or men of a lifeless, formal religion. We are grieved at the sight, and should greatly rejoice if by any means we might convince some that there is a better religion to be attained, a religion worthy of God that gave it. And this we conceive to be no other than love: the love of God and of all mankind; the loving God with all our heart and soul and strength, as having first loved us, as the fountain of all the good we have received, and of all we ever hope to enjoy; and the loving every soul which God hath made, every man on earth, as our own soul.

This love we believe to be the medicine of life, the never-failing remedy, for all the evils of a disordered world, for all the miseries and vices of men. Wherever this is, there are virtue and happiness, going hand in hand. There is humbleness of mind, gentleness, longsuffering, the whole image of God, and at the same time a "peace that passeth all understanding," and "joy unspeakable and full of glory"....

This is the religion we long to see established in the world, a religion of love and joy and peace, having its seat in the heart, in the inmost soul, but ever showing itself by its fruits, continually springing forth not only in all innocence for 'love worketh no ill to his neighbour' but likewise in every kind of beneficence, in spreading virtue and happiness all around it.[23]

The good doctor Wesley properly diagnosed the social disease destroying his nation and God's world. By God's grace he also discovered for himself and for others the "good infection" that could change a human heart and redeem a lost world. This "salvation" was larger than some cared to believe. It was inclusive, not exclusive. It broke down the dividing walls established by "flesh" and erected a new temple not built with hands but composed of living stones.

By salvation I mean, not barely (according to the vulgar notion) deliverance from hell, or going to heaven, but a present deliverance from sin, a restoration of the soul to its primitive health, its original purity; a recovery of the divine nature; the renewal of our souls after the image of God in righteousness and true holiness, in justice, mercy, and truth.... Without faith we cannot be thus saved. For we can't rightly serve God unless we love him. And we can't love him unless we know him; neither can we know God, unless by faith. Therefore salvation by faith is only, in other words, the love of God by the knowledge of God, or the recovery of the image of God by a true spiritual acquaintance with him....

Justifying faith implies ... a sure trust and confidence that Christ died for *my* sins, that he "loved me and give himself for me." And the moment a penitent sinner believes this, God pardons and absolves him. And as soon as his pardon or justification is witnessed to him by the Holy Ghost, he is saved. He loves God and all mankind. He has "the mind that was in Christ" and power to "walk as he also walked." From that time unless he "make shipwreck of the faith" salvation gradually increases in his soul. For "so is the kingdom of God.". . .

Although no man on earth can explain the *particular manner* wherein the Spirit of God works on the soul, yet whosoever has these fruits cannot but know and *feel* that God has wrought them in his heart. Sometimes he acts more particularly on the understanding. . . . Sometimes he acts on the wills and affections. . . . But however it be expressed, it is certain all true faith, and the whole work of salvation, every good thought, word, and work, is altogether by the operation of the Spirit of God.[24]

This note from the doctor is rather long, but it is also a wonderful summary of the design and the workings of God to infect a sick world with the healing power of the new covenant in the Spirit. In the chapters to follow we examine how this medicine of life has infected a sample of over four thousand persons, with a special concern for learning how we might become better carriers of the good infection.

Perhaps an appropriate way to close these opening two chapters before moving on is to cite a hymn of Charles Wesley, making it our prayer as well as his.

GOD of almighty love, by whose sufficient grace
I lift my heart to things above, and humbly seek thy face.

Through Jesus Christ the just my faint desires receive,
And let me in thy goodness trust, and to thy glory live.

Whatever I say or do, thy glory be my aim;
My offerings all be offered through the ever-blessed name.

Jesus, my single eye be fixed on thee alone:
Thy name be praised on earth, on high, thy will by all be done.

Spirit of faith, inspire my consecrated heart;
Fill me with pure, celestial fire, with all thou hast and art.[25]

CHAPTER THREE

Catching the Faith as Children

"Let the little children come to me, and do not stop them; for it is to such as these that the kingdom belongs."

—Jesus (Matthew 19:14)

Bless the Little Children

With all the emphasis in evangelical Protestant Christianity on possessing a well-reasoned and informed faith, isn't it interesting that Jesus broke through the exclusiveness of being "old enough" when—perhaps remembering his own childhood trip to the Temple—he rebuked his disciples for forbidding parents to bring their children to be blessed and said, "Let the little children come to me." Can children enter the kingdom of God? When is someone old enough to really trust in God, decide to follow Jesus, and catch the good infection?

This isn't an easy question to answer, but over ten thousand individuals have been asked similar questions over the last fifteen years by students at Asbury Theological Seminary in Wilmore, Kentucky.[1] Data tabulated from almost four thousand of these interviews indicate that 24% first responded to God's grace during childhood and claimed to have become Christians before the age of ten. Although more women reported early childhood decisions (25.1%) than did men (19.6%), as can be seen in the graph below, a significant number of both genders would say even young children can trust in God and become carriers of the good infection.

66

Age of Becoming a Christian by Gender
1771 Males   2083 Females

This chapter looks at the spiritual journeys of 870 persons who reported they made their faith decisions before the age of ten, or described a process which enabled them to say they had "always" been Christians. The goal is to let them speak for themselves as they describe: (1) the persons and experiences that most influenced their coming to faith, (2) the content and context of those special decisions they made as children, and (3) the impact of those faith decisions as they moved out of childhood and into their adult lives.

One Story

Sharon[2] always saw her Christian testimony as boring. There was nothing special or inspiring about it at all; and in fact, she could not remember a time when she wasn't a Christian, nor could she recall any specific "conversion" experience. She always enjoyed going to church, always felt part of the congregation, and knew early on that she believed the things they believed.

Sharon grew up on a farm in Ohio with both her parents and her grandparents serving as strong role models of faith. They all lived between the earth and God, constantly dependent upon the graciousness of the Lord as they dealt with factors beyond their control. She recalled time after time when her family shared everything they had with others in need. Her grandparents and other members of her extended family served as affirmations of the strong character and deep faith she saw in her parents. Her grandmother was a "great prayer warrior" and Sharon felt her grandmother's prayers had much to do with her understanding of God.

There was a time later in life when Sharon felt her faith being tested—a life-threatening illness, depression, questions about God's will and way—but she found her way through the "valley" resting in the love she had known from a lifelong relationship with God. Two special experiences while she was in her forties also served to confirm and strengthen her faith. She decided to take a break from her career as a teacher to devote more time to her family. This new freedom gave her an opportunity to become more involved in ministry to others. She volunteered to teach a Bible study for college students. This special sense of being used by God produced great satisfaction and joy, and later she felt a call by God to return to teaching and to be a witness for Christ and a source of love for the children in her classroom. Her goal in life at this point is to be more and more Christlike and be an effective witness, especially to her students.

Childhood Agents of Contagion

There is little doubt that parents shape the course of their children's values and life experiences more than any other persons. Almost all of us can remember special incidents with teachers, grandparents, cousins, uncles and aunts, and special playmates in those years between birth and ten. But when it comes to identifying the persons who most influence our faith in God and our commitment to Christ, parents rise to the top of the list.

Several questions on the survey probed early childhood experiences to determine parental roles in faith development. The subjects were asked: (1) how frequently they were involved in church with their family during childhood, (2) what influence church attendance had on their faith, (3) to what extent their parents modeled a life of faith and religious convictions, and (4) who most influenced their desire to become a Christian.

The Importance of Church Involvement

Eighty-nine percent of persons who reported they had "always" been Christians indicated their family involvement in church when they were children was at least monthly, with most (72%) saying it was several times a month. For those who remembered a time of becoming a Christian between the ages of five and nine, 93% said they were actively involved in church with at least one family member during their childhood, with 82% saying they attended several times a month. These statistics are no surprise, with the possible exception that the *always* and *under five* Christians have a lower level of early childhood church involvement than do the *five to nine* Christians. Possible explanations of this pattern will be examined later; but more to the point, early childhood church involvement appears to be an important factor in enabling children to identify themselves as Christians at an early age.

Curious to see the kind of impact this early childhood church attendance had, the interviewers asked the subjects to describe the influence on a sliding scale from strongly negative to strongly positive. Eighty-nine percent of the *always* group reported the experience as either positive or strongly positive (positive—42.9%, strongly positive—46.5%). Among the *five to nine* group 93% reported a positive to strongly positive experience (positive—36.4%, strongly positive—56.7%). Overwhelmingly, children who make early childhood decisions to identify their lives with church and with Christ, remember their early church experience as positive.

Parental Faith Modeling

In addition to church attendance, persons were asked to indicate the degree of parental faith modeling they experienced in childhood. Faith modeling was defined as more than church attendance and included such activities as Bible reading, Bible quoting, regular times of prayer, references to God and/or Christian values during daily conversation, and intentional efforts to live lives faithful to these values. Like Sharon, whose story was shared above, 91% of the *always* Christian group reported they experienced average to significant parental faith modeling. Of those who became Christians between ages five and nine, 89% reported average or significant faith modeling. The only significant difference between these two groups was in the percentage citing "significant" parental faith modeling. Sixty-six percent of the *always* Christian group indicated that they had significant parental faith modeling, while 72% of the *five to nine* group did so. Like early childhood church involvement, parental faith modeling appears to be an important ingredient in children coming to Christian faith before reaching the age of ten.

Agents of Christian Desire

At this point it certainly would not be a surprise to discover that parents are most influential in leading their children to make choices about living a Christian life. When asked which person most influenced their desire to become a Christian, the *always* group reported as follows: both parents—45.0%, mother—16.4%, father—4.8%, and another relative—9.5%. The *five to nine* group had similar answers: Both parents—36.2%, mother—18.3%, father—7.6%, and another relative—5.7%.

Childhood Agents of Desire

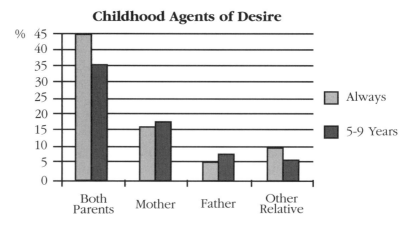

Further analysis of the "other relative" category indicates a "grandmother" as most important. One interesting difference between the two groups occurs in the importance of a Sunday school teacher to this process. Only 1.6% of the *always* group reported that a Sunday school teacher was most important in creating the desire to be a Christian, but 6.5% of those who became Christians between the ages of five and ten did so. The social network widens as we grow older, and the influence of "significant others" beyond the nuclear family becomes more and more important.

When given a chance to explain what it was about their parents that most influenced their interest in living the Christian life, both groups agreed that the most important quality was their obvious "relationship with God" (31.5% and 35.7% respectively). The *always* group listed other important characteristics in the following order: how they cared for me—22.7%, their character/personality—22.1%, and how they cared for others—11.6%. The *five to nine group* answered: their character/personality—23.4%, how they cared for me—13.9%, and how they explained the Bible—12.9%. Again, and in keeping with what was seen earlier in parental faith modeling, there are no surprises. But it is important to recognize that children who themselves make faith decisions recognize that the most lasting impressions made by adults who influence them are memories of persons who loved God, cared for children and others, and revealed the kind of character and personality that made loving God and following Jesus seem attractive. And as these children mature, they find it more and more important that their parents and other adults who influence them can articulate the meaning of the Bible as God's word to children of all ages.

Agents of Christian Decision

Although it is often the case that the persons who most influence our spiritual desires also most influence our spiritual decisions, a separate question was asked of all the subjects to determine if another person emerged as the one helping them come to a clear decision about their faith. The differences, even at an early age, are quite interesting. Among the *always* Christian group—indicating they remembered no particular event of becoming Christians—the results were: both parents—20.2%, mother—17.4%, father—4.5%, as well as pastor—10.1%, evangelist—2.8%, and Sunday school teacher—3.9%. In the *five to nine* group the percentages showed a couple of interesting variations: both parents—13.9%, mother—14.9%, father—7.6%, and (note the shift to) pastor—15.1%, evangelist—11.8%, and Sunday school teacher—9.0%.

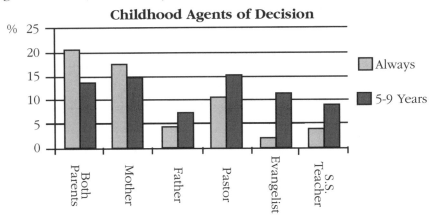

As children enter school and become more acquainted with non-parental adult leaders, apparently they are more and more willing to respond to these leaders and their invitations to Christian decisions and discipleship.

Another interesting shift shows up when the subjects were asked to identify the qualities they remembered about the persons who led them to make faith decisions. The *always* group reported: their relationship with God—27.3%, how they cared for me—23.6%, their character/personality—14.5%, their insistence that I decide—14.5%, and how they explained the Bible—12.1%. The *five to nine* group answered: how they explained the Bible—28.6%, their relationship with God—25.5%, how they cared for me—15.4%, their character/personality—15.1%, and their insistence that I decide—11.4%. Although a vital relationship with God and a loving personality are still critical, it becomes increasingly significant that persons who lead others to Christ—even little children and especially school age children—are able to clarify what the Bible has to say and why it is important that each one of us decides for himself or herself regarding the gift of God's eternal love and life offered through faith in God's Son.

So who are the persons most influencing children to make important faith decisions? To begin with, parents influence them, and especially mothers. It is primarily the lives these parents live and how they display their love for God and for their children that impacts the lives of their sons and daughters. Children from such families are likely to be involved in church activities and remember these as significant and positive experiences. As these boys and girls grow older, additional persons and especially those seen as "other authority figures" including grandmothers, pastors and Sunday school teachers become important to the process of choosing to live the Christian life. And as they make these choices, the faith modeling needed by agents of the gospel includes the ability to explain the Bible and the meaning of becoming a Christian. This communication of the content of the gospel along with a modeling of the character of the gospel makes a personal decision both attractive and possible.

What Do Children Catch?

Depending on our own experience and the testimony of others (whether written or oral), we are sometimes tempted to think that religious decisions made in early childhood are emotional, shallow, and without lasting significance. Is this an accurate evaluation? What do those who themselves made childhood faith decisions report as the meaning and impact of their choices and experiences?

The Anticipated Benefit

When asked what they remembered as their purpose or goal in making the decision, or what it was that they were seeking, they responded in ranked order as follows. Those who were part of the *always* group said: (1) a relationship with God—23.7%, (2) nothing in particular remembered—15.6%, (3) acceptance and love—11.8%, (4) heaven—10.8%, and (5) salvation from sin and guilt—9.1%. Those who were part of the *five to nine* group answered: (1) a relationship with God—21.4%, (2) heaven—21.1%, (3) salvation from sin and guilt—15.7%, (4) nothing in particular remembered, and (5) acceptance and love—8.3%.

It is important to remember that those who reported themselves as *always* having been Christians were not necessarily remembering any particular event from childhood, thus making it difficult if not impossible to accurately describe what was being requested by this question. Note however, that only 20% of the *always* group indicated that obtaining heaven, or salvation from sin and guilt were primary goals of their early childhood faith. In contrast, the *five to nine* group report these two goals almost 37% of the time. This may say something both about the way the gospel is presented to these children and something about the concrete conceptual categories they use for processing sometimes complex ideas. For most of these young kingdom carriers, however, the meaning of their relationship with God continues to expand as they mature and face new challenges and experience new dimensions of grace and power.

Dorris grew up in a poor family in south Georgia. Her parents did not attend church and her father was disillusioned with Christians. Her mother, however, though she worked on Sundays and did not attend church, had a deep love for God and actually helped Dorris find her way to church. A local Baptist congregation sent a bus around to gather up the neighborhood children, and Dorris began to attend as often as she could. She always looked forward to Sundays even though she said this Baptist church was pretty "pushy" about getting saved and accepting Christ. One Sunday when she was eight, children's church met outside under a tree. At the end of the morning the teacher asked all the children to bow their heads and pray. Then she asked if there were any who wanted to ask Jesus into their hearts. Dorris raised her hand and the teacher helped her pray. She knew she wasn't a bad girl, but she had felt a growing sense of conviction of her sins. She wanted to be forgiven and safe ("saved") in Jesus. This is what she found when making her decision for Christ. Her life has had its share of troubles, including several relational and family problems, but in recent years her baptism in the Holy Spirit has enlarged her faith beyond anything she ever dreamed. Above all today, she wants to be faithful and obedient to God's will.

The Leading of God

Did they have any special sense of being led by God when they made their decisions to believe in Christ and be "saved" (the most common expression used by persons reporting childhood faith decisions)? Presented in ranked order the *always* group answered: (1) just family influence—28.0%, (2) a growing conviction—20.4%, (3) nothing remembered—19.4%, (4) a gradual quest—8.1%, and (5) a crisis faced—8.1%. The *five to nine* group shared the following answers: (1) a growing conviction—23.2%, (2) just family influence—17.6%, (3) nothing remembered—17.6%, (4) something special that was read or said—11.4%, and (5) a gradual quest—8.2%.

It is a lot to ask of adults, especially older adults, that they try to remember what was happening in their lives as children when they made critical faith decisions. What is clear is that most believed they were just living out their own identity as members of a faith family and responding to a gradual awareness that they had to make a faith decision of their own. Some remembered a special story or explanation of the gospel, but the sense of being led by God is primarily a matter of family relationships and not any special moment of truth or conviction.

The Message Remembered

Although those reporting they were "saved" or "accepted Christ"[3] as children had very little recollection of a particular message being read or spoken, this does not mean they had no awareness of the

74

general meaning of the gospel message. When asked what aspect of the gospel was most important to them as they made their Christian decisions, the *always* group responded: (1) God's love, grace, and acceptance—24.2%, (2) nothing remembered—18.3%, (3) the person sharing with me was the message—9.7%, (4) assurance of going to heaven—8.6%, and (5) the possibility of knowing God—8.1%. The *five to nine* group answered: (1) nothing remembered—21.2%, (2) God's love, grace, and acceptance—19.2%, (3) assurance of going to heaven—14.9%, (4) avoiding God's wrath, judgment, and punishment—8.2%, and (5) the possibility of knowing God—7.8%

The only surprise might be the appearance of item four in about 8% of the *five to nine* group. But again, "salvation" is from something and to something (or "someone," a tremendously important distinction apparently recognized even by most children). When children grasp the reality of attaining heaven as one significant aspect of the gospel, it should not be surprising that the consequence of not attaining heaven is closely linked in their minds. After all, Jesus said he came to seek and to save the "lost." Even children can begin to recognize that being lost—a very real and terrifying danger experienced sooner or later by most children—is worth every effort to avoid. Likewise, nearly every child has experienced the wrath and punishment of an earthly parent, and they know enough to seek a way to avoid such consequences. In a sense, the real surprise is that these categories of the gospel message occupy such a low percentage of memory. It will be interesting to note what differences of emphasis appear in the ages and stages examined later.

The Experience Itself

When asked if they remembered this decision time as mostly an emotional experience or mostly a matter of new insight, little difference is found between the two groups. Although some might expect that children make "emotional" faith decisions, in fact 51.1% report that they remember it as a balanced or evenly mixed (emotion and insight) decision, 23.2% report it as mostly insight, and only 25.7% report it as mostly an emotional experience. Those who were part of the *five to nine* group were slightly more likely to remember it as an emotional decision (26.8% compared to 22.1%). At this point we are not comparing these results with other groups, and thus about all that can be said is that adults who remember their childhood faith decisions see them as a mixture of insight and emotions.

When asked to describe these insights or emotions they responded as follows. Those in the *always* group reported: (1) peace, relaxation, and/or contentment—18.4%, (2) joy, happiness, and/or excitement—16.8%, and (3) acceptance, love, and/or belonging—13.4%. The *five to nine* group answered: (1) joy, happiness, and/or excitement—22.5%, (2) peace, relaxation, and/or contentment—15.0%, (3-tie) acceptance, love, and/or belonging—12.7%, (3-tie) relief, release, and/or freedom—12.7%, and (5) cleansed, forgiven—6.0%. There emerges only a slight indication that children who make Christian faith decisions are dealing with issues of remorse or repentance related to sin and guilt as they move into their later childhood. This raises questions regarding the nature of their "saving" faith and how their faith will carry them as they move into the troubling years of adolescence.

What Are the Lasting Effects?

Do children who grow up in strong Christian homes and make early Christian faith decisions have more or less difficulty adjusting to life's challenges as they move along through adolescence and adulthood? What kinds of additional faith experiences have they had? What are their longings and perspectives on life, their world, and their faith today? These are the questions explored in the final section of the interview format.

Crises Faced

The subjects were asked if they had experienced any crises of faith following their faith decisions. Had their faith been tested? Had they struggled with holding on to their faith? Up to three responses were able to be recorded. Some reported no major struggles or problems, others recounted several.

With one exception, the two groups were within a few percentage points of each other on their answers. The major exception was in a category often summarized as "a time of backsliding[4] and recommitment." While 24.0% of the *always* group reported having faced this crisis of faith, almost four in ten (38.4%) of the subjects in the *five to nine* group indicated this was their experience. Other "crises of faith" reported by these groups as they moved through life can be seen in the table below.

Table 1

Crises of Faith Most Commonly Reported

Responses Ranked by Overall Childhood Frequency	Always	Ages 5-9
(1) "backsliding"	24.0%	38.4%
(2) "marriage, family, relationships"	28.0%	28.9%
(3) "God's call on my life"	24.0%	29.1%
(4) "doubt and confusion"	24.5%	28.2%
(5) "death of friend/family member"	27.5%	22.0%
(6) "career and job decisions"	24.5%	18.1%
(7) "disillusionment with Christians"	18.0%	18.4%
(8) "other crises mentioned"	11.0%	13.8%

Perhaps the most important observation to make is that many of us face the same challenges to our faith as we move through life. It is yet to be seen how the crisis of "backsliding" experienced by so many of those who made early childhood decisions compares with other groups, but it is obvious that many children are going to face this challenge. How they will succeed in the recovery process our subjects described will be determined largely by who is available to them later in life—often in their early adult years—as faith models and persons who can answer their questions and help heal their hurts.

Additional Episodes

Opportunity was provided for all of the subjects to identify other significant faith experiences beyond what they normally would describe as "becoming a Christian." Again, as in the previous question, up to three such special events, processes, or meaningful moments could be recorded. The most frequently mentioned cate-

77

gory by both groups was "nothing special, just gradual growth" which was mentioned by 48.8% of the *always* group and 35.8% of the *five to nine* group. It is difficult to evaluate this response. Perhaps we live in a society where nothing is expected beyond "claiming of our faith" and living it out as faithful church members. Perhaps, especially among those who have "always" been Christians, there is no expectation for profoundly meaningful encounters with God or the arrival of a wonderful new insight to living out our Christian faith. If so, we may well ask if the church has in some ways failed in its witness to those who have no "sacred moments." Or, it may be that these very things are thought of as "nothing special, just the expected occurrences of gradual growth." This remains something of a mystery and will need further clarification.

There were, however, other spiritual encounters and special moments remembered by those who claimed early childhood as their time of coming to Christian faith.

Table 2

Additional Faith Experiences Most Commonly Reported

Responses Ranked by Overall Childhood Frequency	Always	Ages 5-9
(1) "nothing special, gradual growth"	48.8%	35.8%
(2) "water baptism"	31.5%	35.5%
(3) "God's call to a special ministry"	28.0%	32.3%
(4) "Holy Spirit baptism or filling"	18.5%	26.6%
(5) "experience of sanctification"	9.0%	19.0%
(6) "experience of healing"	12.5%	15.6%
(7) "other meaningful experience"	15.0%	14.7%
(8) "another conversion or restoration"	7.5%	12.0%

In light of the fact that most of these persons would probably have experienced water baptism (if they could remember it at all) close to the time of their initial faith experience, it is not surprising that they recall this as a very special additional faith experience. Perhaps we make too little of baptism. It is too often, I fear, a brief and ritualistic event without the drama and power of divine encounter that ought to be expected in the mystery of this once-in-a-lifetime sacrament.[5] Even if the Christian initiate involved in this holy moment be a child, the baptismal event apparently carries with it a lasting and precious memory.

Perhaps one of the most surprising discoveries is the fact that 28% to 32% of these children who grew up in Christian homes and were exposed to dynamic faith modeling and meaningful church activities indicate that they have experienced a call by God to a special ministry. The data provide no detail regarding how this special calling was sensed, processed, or experienced. This remains an area needing additional research. But perhaps many of us who have had a similar nudge from the Holy Spirit to "be or do something special for God" (whether lay or clergy) need to be more aware of how to help our young brothers and sisters explore, articulate, and respond to such urgings to be useful to the Lord's work.

Finally, although different denominations and traditions use various expressions to describe the "second work of grace" or the encounter of the Christian believer with the Holy Spirit's claim on our lives for full surrender and "filling," it is encouraging to see that 27.5% of the *always* group and 46.5% of the *five to nine* group recall either an experience of "Holy Spirit baptism or filling" and/or "sanctification." What this actually means to those who claim such significant encounters with the Spirit of God should be explored much more fully. In reality, the grouping of the these "Holy Spirit" encounters into one category is not entirely appropriate. Too much is at stake to allow these critical experiences to be loosely clumped together as identical. However, they are at least similar, and indicate that the purpose of God as declared in Saint Peter's first sermon— "and you shall receive the gift of the Holy Spirit"[6]—is more at work in the lives of some of our church members than we might know. We will look at this more closely in Chapter 5.

Concerns for Today

The final question asked in the interviews was "As a Christian, what are your greatest longings or concerns today?" It was left open to be interpreted however they might, but the intent was to emphasize "As a Christian . . . ." Their answers after being grouped and categorized were:

Table 3

Concerns Most Commonly Reported

Responses Ranked by Overall Childhood Frequency	Always	Ages 5-9
(1) "to grow in the Lord"	34.0%	45.4%
(2) "be a better witness to others"	28.5%	31.0%
(3) "to serve God with my life"	24.5%	28.1%
(4) "better devotional and prayer life"	21.5%	28.5%
(5) "to know God's will"	22.5%	23.8%
(6) "sanctification/Christlikeness"	16.0%	20.6%
(7) "change in the Church"	18.5%	19.3%
(8) "justice, peace, hope for world"	21.0%	9.6%

The most obvious concerns and longings are related to areas of personal spiritual growth and faithfulness. About 30% indicate a desire to be more useful to God through faithful service and Christian witness, and about 20% are concerned about the health of their churches or the Church in general. Perhaps the most interesting contrast between the *always* group and the *five to nine* group is seen in the lack of concern among the latter for more justice and peace in the world. At this point there is no obvious answer for the disparity. It does raise the question, however, as to whether or not emphasizing personal salvation for children under the age of ten contributes to a lack of social focus in their understanding of themselves as Christians. Just a thought worthy of more thorough evaluation.

A Synopsis

Several interesting observations can be made. Based on the sample interviewed, over 20% of Americans who affirm that they are Christians arrive at that realization before the age of ten. These persons have strong parental faith modeling and positive childhood experiences in church. They are moved toward claiming their own faith by the Christian love they see manifested by parents and other adult family members, especially mothers and grandmothers.

Those who recall a specific time when they became Christians say that in addition to the love and faith manifested by their spiritual guides, these agents possessed the ability to explain the message of the Bible and clarify how to appropriate it. Most remember this gospel as an offer to know more about God's love and acceptance and say they had been gradually led to the conviction that they needed this special relationship with God offered through Jesus. Their experience at the time of making this decision was a joyous one filled with peace and happiness. Yet most are quite certain it was not just an emotional moment, but a decision made based on insight and special feelings.

One of the most challenging spiritual problems faced later in life by those who make early childhood decisions for Christ, is what has sometimes been called the experience of "falling away" or "back-sliding." Nearly 40%[7] say that they have gone through a season when they abandoned or at least seriously neglected their relationship with God. Problems with relationships and fitting their childhood faith into life's disappointments seemed to be the greatest contributors to this "slip-sliding away." Nevertheless, those interviewed in this survey were able to find their way back and many have even felt a call to a special ministry for God. Perhaps part of this recovery of faith is related to their discovery of the active presence and power of the third person of the Trinity. It is not surprising that now they want to grow in their faith, see the church become more vibrant, and be better faith models for others in their witnessing and service. Of course, all of their stories are not as rosy as this summary might indicate. They still struggle. But as adults they long to find new meaning for their childhood faith, and reveal in their own lives more of the faithful discipleship they remember in the lives of those who shaped their early journey toward God.

Additional Observations

It seems worth noting that more than likely some of the differences reflected in the personal stories examined above result from the various denominational backgrounds represented. For example, one would think that Roman Catholics would have much more difficulty trying to identify when they were "saved" or "became Christians" than would Southern Baptists. Since the subjects interviewed were asked to identify both their present denomination and the denomination of their childhood, perhaps some light can be shed on this matter.

Staying with the example above, it is interesting that only 11.5% (the third-highest percentage recorded after Friends and Wesleyans) of those with early Roman Catholic affiliation (208 persons) indicated that they thought of themselves as having "always" been Christians. On the other hand, 34.6% (five times as high a percentage as any other denomination sampled) of those who presently identified themselves as Roman Catholic (fifty-two persons) indicated that they had always been Christians. We might say that if Catholics remain Catholics, about one third of them think of themselves as having always been Christians. If however, they "fall away" and later become affiliated with some other denomination, they are much less likely to claim that they have "always" been Christians.

On the other side of this childhood denomination issue, it would seem obvious that persons with a Salvation Army background[8] would not rank "water baptism" very high on their list of "additional faith experiences" and that Baptists would. That is exactly what is found, with only 5.6% of those having early Salvation Army orientation listing this as a meaningful additional experience and 41.8% of Baptists doing so. But there are also some surprises. One might think that persons raised in the conservative yet socially active arena of the Salvation Army would be more likely to express a concern for greater "justice, peace, and hope for the world." In reality, they ranked lowest of all denominations with only 2.7%, while persons with early Free Methodist and Roman Catholic affiliations ranked near the top with 18.9% and 15.9% respectively. Current Roman Catholics move to the top in commitment to this concern (32.7%) while Free Methodists drop slightly to 14.5% (ranked fifth, behind Catholics, Lutherans, Presbyterians, and those without a present denominational affiliation). Some issues seemingly important to the denominations that influence us in childhood are apparently not caught (even if taught) until later in life.

A second observation has to do with the fact that more and more persons in America today are changing denominational affiliation as they move away from home and through life's stages. Although this study has significant limits both in terms of representing a stratified random sample of all Christians in the United States,[9] and in terms of its denominational diversity,[10] it nevertheless reveals a significant openness on the part of many of those interviewed to "shift loyalties." In this study, largely focused on denominations related to the Wesleyan-Arminian family, it is not surprising that Lutherans (87%), Roman Catholics (81%), Presbyterians (80%), and Baptists (65%) were most commonly found to have shifted denominations. But almost all denominations surveyed showed significant shifts. Sixty-four percent of Friends (Quakers) reported they changed denominations, followed by Nazarenes (61%), "other" (the catchall and thus perhaps the most generic category—54%), and Pentecostals (54%). According to this study, the Free Methodists were best at keeping their members with only 19% reporting having changed from that childhood denomination.

We do live in a different world than the one many of us grew up in, or thought we grew up in. Mobility related to education and occupation is certainly a major part of this world, but so is mobility related to church affiliation. Effective and growing congregations recognize this and make the necessary adjustments to invite persons from "other" backgrounds to join them for the critical "next stage" of their Christian journey without communicating to them "you are not one of us." Rather, they try to communicate "We're interested in you and what God has been doing in your life. Come join us as we grow together and look for new ways to be more committed to all that God has for us as children of God and disciples of Jesus Christ." The contagious faith caught in childhood is not restricted to a single strain. It is able to show up again later in life and be incubated in a new Christian community manifesting somewhat different qualities than the original, but nevertheless revealing the reality of God's transforming presence and stimulating the continued growth of *the good infection*.

> Child of blessing, child of promise, baptized with the Spirit's sign;
>   with this water God has sealed you unto love and grace divine.
> Child of love, our love's expression, love's creation, loved indeed!
> Fresh from God, refresh our spirits, into joy and laughter lead.
> Child of joy, our dearest treasure, God's you are, from God you
>   came.
> Back to God we humbly give you; live as one who bears Christ's
>   name.
> Child of God your loving Parent, learn to know whose child you are.
> Grow to laugh and sing and worship, trust and love God more than
>   all.[11]

CHAPTER FOUR

The Susceptible Years— Adolescence

"Susceptible—capable of receiving, admitting, undergoing, or being affected by something."
— *Webster's Encyclopedic Unabridged Dictionary*
of the English Language

Persons remembering the time when they responded to God's personal invitation in Jesus Christ often describe a period in their lives filled with turmoil and troubling. Although we might prefer it otherwise, these times of "crisis" sooner or later come to us all as part of the condition of being alive. Sometimes, like Ebenezer Scrooge, we are afraid to face these interrupting spirits, and simply wait and hope for the dawn of a new day when they will disappear around the corners of our private histories and once more we will have escaped—though without any sense of respite. But such seasons of susceptibility are always potential occasions for hearing the voice of God, acknowledging our need for amazing grace, and catching the good infection. This chapter takes a look at one of these seasons: adolescence.

The "Conversion" Boom

When William James (physician, chemist, psychologist, philosopher) was asked to give the Gifford Lectures on Natural Religion at the University of Edinburgh in 1901, he had already achieved "an international reputation as America's most original thinker since

Jonathan Edwards."[1] His century-old study of conversion and religious experience is still must reading for all who seek to understand the workings of the human soul in response to God. James, unfortunately opting for the psychological interpretations of his day, designated the two paths to religious conviction as the "healthy minded" approach and the "sick soul" approach. According to James, persons fitting into the "healthy minded" or "once born" pattern to happiness, see the world as a place in which they merely need to tally the pluses and minuses, and decide to live on the plus side. Those he designates as "sick souls" or "twice borns" have "an incompletely unified moral and intellectual constitution"[2] and require a "straightening out and unifying of the inner self"[3] in order to find health and happiness. It is this second group and their "conversions," whether gradual or sudden,[4] which were of special interest to James and a host of other psychologists, sociologists, and practical theologians who have followed in his footsteps.

Actually a predecessor of William James, Edwin D. Starbuck, is the one who first collected (1898) and then published (1906) data from 1,265 case studies[5] and noticed the pronounced correlation between adolescence and conversion. The average age reported by Starbuck for conversion among his sample was 16.4 years of age. Other studies followed and affirmed that the average age for conversion ranged from 16.6 to 12.7.[6] When are persons most likely to become fully aware of and committed to their faith in God? The most common answer is when they are in transition from childhood to the responsibilities and obligations of being adults; a time normally referred to as adolescence.

Jesus was twelve (Luke 2:42-52) when he felt the irresistible urge to uncover his own unique spiritual identity. While on pilgrimage to Jerusalem, he wandered away from his family and found his way into the Temple. There he sat among the teachers for hours on end asking probing questions, and there he first claimed to his exasperated parents his special identity as a child of his heavenly Father. Many cultures recognize this major season of claiming one's own identity and "coming of age" through rites of passage. Western society has tended to minimize these rites, but this is still the most common season of susceptibility to experiencing God's special presence and claiming a new identity as a child of God.

Drawing on data from nearly four thousand of the ten thousand spiritual inventories generated by the Asbury study, it is clear that adolescence[7] is still the most common time frame for making initial Christian decisions and experiencing Christian conversion.

Age of Becoming a Christian by Gender

1771 Males   2083 Females

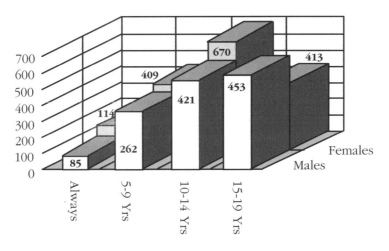

According to the interviews, 28% of all subjects first responded to God's grace during early adolescence (age ten to fourteen). Another 23% remembered making their initial decision for Christ after they were fifteen and before the age of twenty. Thus 51% of those who remembered making a Christian decision did so during the decade after they turned ten and before they became twenty. When added to the 23% examined in the last chapter who identify their childhood years as the season of their initial response to the Christian faith, nearly 75% of those interviewed claimed they came to their faith decisions before the age of twenty. Surely this should remind us of the very special attention we ought to be giving to both our children and our youth. But in this chapter, we examine the unique and challenging age usually referred to as youth or adolescence.

Today's Adolescent

In 1999 there were 19.5 million young people in America ten to fourteen years old, and another 19.7 million teenagers fifteen to nineteen. All together this slice of the American population now totals over thirty-nine million persons.[8] The "baby boom" of the last generation that peaked in the number of children in elementary and secondary schools in 1971 is peaking again. In 1997 the total number of children in grades K-12 surpassed the figures of 1971 for the first time, and the trend should continue into the new century. But there are changes. Seldom a week goes by without a new article in the printed news media and a corresponding "special" on TV describing the challenges of growing up in today's world. Being a young person in transition from childhood to adulthood is without doubt more and more challenging.[9] Almost none of us who have made it "around the corner"—or over the hill, as some would say— have any desire to go back and relive those days, no matter how enchanting we try to make them sound by playing the "oldies." But regardless of the era, the social context, or the name assigned to any particular generation, dealing with one's own identity, sexuality, and peer group makes adolescence a season of both danger and opportunity.

Early Adolescence

Actually, it is not easy to define exactly when adolescence begins, in part because it is different for each person, and because it is gender specific. For most it begins during what we in the United States call the years of middle high or junior high school. Although studies indicate that the first menstrual period for girls begins on average during year twelve, the female growth spurt of physical change begins before the age of ten. Boys follow along on average about two to three years later.

Wayne Rice has given his life to ministry aimed at this early adolescent age group. In his book *Junior High Ministry* he cites a summary by Don Wells, principal of the Carolina Friends School, concerning the issues faced by this age group, and the challenges this creates for teachers and other adults working with them.

1. *Fact:* Early adolescents need to try on a wide variety of roles.
2. *Fact:* Early adolescents vary enormously . . . in physical, mental and emotional maturity and capability.
3. *Fact:* During early adolescence the development of control over one's life through conscious decision-making is crucial.
4. *Fact:* Early adolescence is an age where all natural forces (muscular, intellectual, glandular, emotional) are causing peaks and troughs in their entire being.

5. *Fact:* Early adolescents need space and experience to "be" different persons at different times.
6. *Fact:* Early adolescents are preoccupied by physical and sexual concerns, frightened by their perceived inadequacy.
7. *Fact:* Early adolescents need a distinct feeling of present importance, a present relevancy of their own lives now.[10]

The pressure is on to grow up. What does that mean for spiritual development? Rice says there are eight characteristics of "junior high spirituality."
1. It is a faith in transition.
2. It includes doubt and disbelief.
3. It is personal.
4. It includes feelings.
5. It is difficult for junior highers to put into practice.
6. It includes failure.
7. It is idealistic.
8. It needs models.[11]

Those who are presently watching their own children move through these in-between years, and those who can remember their own early adolescent forays into faith recognize the accuracy of these observations. Yet, it is under these wildly unstable times that more persons say they put their trust in the Rock of God's Salvation (28%), than during any other time of their lives. In this chapter, 1,091 persons, 670 female and 421 male, describe some of the influences and experiences they remember from faith decisions made during early adolescence.

Late Adolescence

Normally when we hear the word "teenagers" we think of young people in late adolescence, or between the years of fifteen and nineteen. The physical-psychological-emotional changes and pressures to choose, which began in early adolescence accelerate during the last half of this decade of development. MTV, the Internet, a driver's license, expensive designer clothes, increased competition between the authority of parent(s) and peers, and the pressures of school, job, romance, and "belonging" make this stage of growing up an adventure full of both promise and peril. An increasing number of youth in this season of life aren't making it through the gauntlet. Suicide, murder, accidents, AIDS, and overdoses seem to claim more and more lives each year. Late adolescence is a time of walking a tightrope stretched between self-expression and self-control.

David Breskin, writing in an article for *Rolling Stone* entitled "Dear Mom and Dad," described the challenge as follows.

> Chances are an adolescent's parents are divorced.... Married or divorced, the adolescent's mother works outside the home.... That the father is absent or away at work is a given. By the time [he] graduates from high school, he'll have spent more time with his blue flickering electronic parent than anything else but sleeping.
>
> While he's a teenager, [his parents] spend an average of 14 minutes a week communicating with him. He has more access to booze, dope, pills, coke, than any previous generation of kids, and at an earlier age.... Chances are increasing that he'll be sexually or physically assaulted by an adult at an early age.[12]

These are the pressures. Most teenagers make it through, and most in the United States have a modicum of religious faith. George Gallup reports that 95% of America's youth believe in God and 93% say they believe God loves them.[13] Yet most of these, including many who attend church regularly, seem to have only a thin veneer of religion bearing little resemblance to biblical Christianity[14] and hardly any awareness that the gospel is about an intimate relationship with the God of grace and justice instead of about old-fashioned rules and regulations designed to spoil a good time. Only 29% report they have ever had any experience of the presence of God.[15] Gallup writes:

> Survey findings clearly reveal that young people today are in some respects surprisingly religious. At the same time, it should be carefully noted that religious faith does not have primacy in the lives of some and that many are turned off by churches and organized religion. Evidence that churches are failing to play a central role in the religious lives of many youth is seen in the following:
>
> Less than half of America's teens (43%) believe it is very important to have a deep religious faith.... [It] ranks only eighth as being very important on a list of nine values tested.... Only 13 percent of the teens interviewed feel that religion has a great deal of influence; an additional 30 percent say it has some influence, and another 28 percent feel it has very little influence. Only one teen in four expresses a high degree of confidence in organized religion.[16]

Similarly, a University of Michigan study indicated in 1980 that 65% of high school seniors said religion was important or very important in their lives, and 43% reported that they were involved weekly in religious services. By 1994 these figures had dropped to 58% and 32% respectively.[17] Nevertheless, it is during this late adolescence period that 22.5% of those in our study (866 persons, 413 females and 453 males), second only to the numbers in early adolescence, see themselves as having made a deep and lasting "Christian decision." Most of them have discovered what studies indicate, "that the closer people feel to God, the better they feel about themselves. They are also satisfied with their lives more than are others; they are more altruistic; they enjoy better health and have a happier outlook."[18]

One Story

Kip attended church almost weekly when he was growing up. His parents were both deeply involved in their church and modeled their Christian convictions and contagious faith to Kip and others. A new pastor arrived, and Kip's parents took it upon themselves not only to welcome him but to become his friends. It was this friendship with a minister that most profoundly changed Kip's perception of Christianity. Prior to becoming acquainted with his new pastor, Kip perceived Christianity as "dullness and duty" with no room for "enjoyment and humor." But he began to see that being a Christian could be "just plain fun!"

Because he was already confirmed as a member of the church, he considered himself to be a Christian. But as a thirteen-year-old teenager he was struggling with some personal habits and felt particular confusion, guilt, and shame because of his cursing and swearing. He felt he was dishonoring Jesus, who died for him. Thus he decided one night in the privacy of his own bedroom to commit his whole life—including these problem areas—to Jesus Christ as his Savior and Lord. Within a week he realized his swearing and cursing habit had been curtailed, and he decided to tell others about his new personal discovery. During an altar call one night at church he went forward and knelt in prayer and then shared with the entire congregation what he had experienced.

Sometimes the faith decisions and discoveries of teenagers don't seem particularly "significant" to adults, or even to those teenagers when they become adults. But moments like Kip experienced in his bedroom and in front of that congregation are just as real and life-shaping as any Damascus Road conversion. Kip was not a "bad" kid, but he came to realize because of a "bad habit" that his Christian faith had to be claimed as a relationship that honored Christ. What is more basic than that?

What then can we learn from examining some of the details of these 1,957 stories of adolescent faith development and conversion?

Who Influences Them?

Following the sequence established in Chapter 3, this section looks at the contagious agents involved in helping young people come to faith discoveries and decisions. Some patterns are quite similar to those we noted among persons becoming Christians as children. Nevertheless, youth have their own special path to the faith they claim as their own.

Church Background and Parental Faith Modeling

As we noted in the last chapter, persons who become Christians as children have had: (1) significant involvement in church as they grew up, and (2) parents who lived out and modeled their faith. The same pattern is present for those making Christian choices as youth, with the exception that the influences are not quite as strong. For example, notice in the table below the declining percentage of persons who say they had average to significant exposure to church as children, positive experiences regarding their church backgrounds, and average to significant parental faith modeling.[19]

Table 4

Age Christian Compared to Positive Childhood Exposure

Age of Becoming Christian	Significant Church Exposure	Positive Church Experience	Significant Faith Modeling
Always	89.0%	89.4%	90.5%
Age 5-9	92.7%	93.1%	88.5%
Age 10-14	82.8%	86.5%	77.5%
Age 15-19	64.1%	66.0%	55.9%
Age 20-24	57.6%	52.3%	47.7%
Age 25-29	48.1%	51.7%	40.2%

The drop is obvious for those in the ten to fourteen age range, but even more pronounced in the fifteen-to-nineteen-year-old converts. For comparison, the table also includes young adults or those coming to a personal Christian faith decision in their twenties.

It appears obvious that the lower the level of family involvement in church and the lower the level of positive faith modeling, the older persons are when they come to a personal faith decision. Simply put, and not at all surprising, parental faith modeling and family attendance at church seem to make a significant difference in how soon we are most likely to "catch" the good infection.

Persons Influencing Desire to Be Christian

Perhaps again a table will help clarify who it is that most influences youth as compared to children when it comes to creating a desire to live their lives as Christians.

Table 5

Age Christian Compared to Persons of Influence

Age of Becoming Christian	Both Parents	Pastor	Youth Leader	Friend or Peer
Always	45.0%	4.2%	3.7%	1.6%
Age 5-9	36.2%	6.5%	2.2%	1.6%
Age 10-14	19.6%	11.9%	7.8%	7.0%
Age 15-19	9.5%	9.4%	11.2%	22.9%

Since the "always" category probably represents a broad range of actual experiences with no single recollection of making a Christian choice, it is only helpful in that again it reminds us of the importance of parents above all others. But note how decidedly different the influence of parents is by the time children reach the age of early adolescence and even more so by the time they reach late adolescence. The role of the pastor increases during the "age of accountability" or "confirmation class," but then drops off again as teens become high schoolers. But perhaps what is most significant is the radical increase of peer influence during late adolescence.

Sociologists have described this shifting pattern of influence for some time. It is therefore probably not a surprise to many of us. Nevertheless, we may be able to recognize in these figures why it is so critical to enlarge the experience of Christian community for our children as they grow older, and especially include opportunities for them to interact with friends who are contagiously Christian.

Hule Goddard and Jorge Acevedo write in their very helpful guide for working with adolescents, *The Heart of Youth Ministry:*

> One of the best ministries we can offer young people is to create for them a group of Christian peers. A Christian peer group is a mirror that reflects back to our young people: "You are worth much—you are valuable to us." This group can generate the unconditional love that is essential for healthy development of one's personality and self-esteem. It can say, "It is okay to be a Christian; it is a good thing to do God's will."[20]

Friends are important to all of us, and especially to adolescents. We are, after all, relational beings designed for the ultimate relationship—friendship with God. It only stands to reason that good friends who are themselves discovering and seeking to live in this reality are better carriers of the good infection to peer-focused teens than anyone else.

When asked what it was about these agents of influence that made the Christian life attractive, the subjects' responses were identical to those given by persons who became Christians as children: (1) "their relationship with God," (2) "their character and personality," (3) "they cared about me," and (4) "they explained the Bible."

Persons Influencing Christian Decision

Sometimes the persons having the greatest impact on our exposure and attitudes about the Christian life are not the ones who actually are involved in helping us come to a faith commitment. In the earlier recounting of Kip's faith journey he gave credit to his pastor as one of the most influential persons in his realization that Christianity was more than he had realized. Yet when he made a deeply personal decision about his own relationship with Christ, he did so alone with God in his bedroom. Kip's pastor was involved in the invitation offered at the Sunday evening service, and Kip did go forward; but he had already made his decision alone with God.

Persons becoming Christians as early adolescents report that their pastors are most important in helping them arrive at their Christian faith decisions (20.3%). Evangelists rank second (13.3%) followed by youth leaders (9.0%), mothers (8.1%), both parents (7.5%), and peers/friends (5.7%). Late adolescents have a slightly different story to tell. They report peers and friends in first place (17.4%), followed by pastors (15.2%), evangelists (12.8%), youth leaders (11.2%), and both parents (2.2%). Once again, the growing significance of peers emerges. As teenagers grow older and move from middle high to senior high, parents—especially fathers[21]—are far less likely to be the ones leading their children to faith decisions. The carriers of the good infection who are most helpful in leading late adolescents to faith discoveries and decisions are peers, pastors, and youth leaders. Why? What seems to make the difference? The 1,769 subjects who made their commitments to Christ as ten- to nineteen-year-old adolescents were asked what it was about these agents of the gospel that enabled them to step across the line to a new discovery of God's reality. As was the case with children, a significant shift takes place. The most important qualities of those helping them to appropriate for themselves the life-changing power of the gospel are: (1) "their ability to explain the biblical message" (early = 26.1%, late = 26.8%) and (2) "their own obvious relationship with God" (early = 27.2%, late = 26.3%). Two other factors likewise rated about the same in significance: (3) "they cared for me" (early = 14.9%, late = 15.7%), and "something about their personality and character" (early = 13.2%, late = 15.5%). Pastors, youth leaders, peers, parents, or any others wishing to lead youth to a life-changing experience of surrender to Christ as Savior and Lord of Life need to be prepared to be watched and questioned.

Peter's advice to Christians in the first century regarding their witness seems an appropriate summary of how these qualities fit together.

1. *In your hearts set apart Christ as Lord.* (#1 above—"obvious relationship with God")
2. *Always be prepared to give an answer to everyone who asks you to give the reason for the hope that you have.* (#2 above—"ability to explain the biblical message")

3. *But do this with gentleness and respect.* (#3 above—"personality, character, cared about me") (1 Peter 3:15, NIV)

How Do They Describe Their Experiences?

Katrina grew up in Estonia, a small country situated across from Finland on the Baltic Sea. Estonia was under the rule of the Soviet Union during much of Katrina's early life and she had no real exposure to religion or the Christian gospel since her parents were members of the Communist Party and atheists. After the 1989 dissolution of the Soviet Union, Katrina and many of her peers began to search for meaning in their lives. At the age of sixteen she started taking classes in a business school and spent some time exploring transcendental meditation. Something was still missing.

Several things began to happen in short period of time which she later saw as God's leading in her life. She became aware of a distant uncle who was a Christian pastor in the United States. She also found her soul deeply moved by reading the life story of Mother Teresa. Then a family of missionaries moved into the home of a non-Christian friend of hers. Her friend warned her about what this new family was teaching, but they needed an interpreter and Katrina was curious.

She began interpreting for the missionaries as they shared the gospel. At the age of seventeen, while translating at a children's camp, Katrina felt led of the Holy Spirit to respond herself to the invitation and give her life to Christ. Her search for purpose in life and a growing desire to personally know God were satisfied as she prayed and experienced a deep sense of release and acceptance, and a whole new level of wonder, meaning, and reality.

Everyone's story is certainly not like Katrina's. But what are the some of the common themes in the stories told by persons who found their way to Christ as adolescents?

The Nature of the Quest

When asked if they could name what they were looking for when they made their decisions, the most common answer for both early and late adolescents was "a relationship with God" (early = 22.8%, late = 22.0%). But following this initial agreement, there are significant differences in what youth are seeking. Early adolescents listed "salvation from sin and guilt" (15.2%) as second, followed by "gaining heaven and avoiding hell" (14.0%), and "filling a void and finding peace" (10.3%). This pattern is generally more like that of children ages five to nine than it is like those who make Christian commitments as older teenagers. Late adolescents are more likely to mention "filling a void and finding peace" (18.7%), "meaning and purpose in life" (13.5%), or "acceptance and love" (11.0%).

Dawson McAllister is a youth communicator and author who has spent more than thirty years of his life listening to and speaking to teenagers. After one recent two-day conference for teens he asked them to write anonymous notes about anything they wanted to say. "Just be honest," he told them. They were. He writes:

> I carried their scribbled notes home in that plastic bag. It's a bag full of pain, more pain than I could have imagined. One note was from a girl who wrote, "Why? Why is everything so hard and painful? A few weeks ago I was raped and told no one. I'm so scared.". . .
>
> Through the years of my ministry I've seen many different hairstyles, clothing styles and types of music. Those things come and go, but some things never change.
>
> The needs of the heart do not change. Teenagers today still need what teenagers have always needed. . . . They still search for answers. And they still respond to truth.[22]

As might be expected, the dominant issues of life shift from early to late adolescence. As teens get older they are less likely to make major faith and life decisions based on traditional religious categories alone such as salvation defined as "going to heaven and escaping hell." They are more interested in finding answers for how to live in this world filled with fleeting relationships, low self esteem, a sense of emptiness, and loss of meaning and direction. They are looking more for a Savior for today than for tomorrow. The gospel offered must address the pain, confusion, and struggle of day-to-day living, not just an offer for an afterlife. They want to know if God is real, and if by truly trusting in Christ they can find "happiness."

The Leading of God

When asked if they sensed any special leading of God to their time of decision and new faith, both groups answered that they primarily sensed God's leading as a "growing conviction" (early = 32.3%, late = 34.1%). About 11% of both groups described it as a "gradual quest," something they had become more and more aware of and interested in as a possibility for their lives. Another 11.6% of the older teens described it as a "hunger for God" and 10% of this group said they sensed God's leading through a "crisis" they were facing. About 9% of both groups felt God had led them to "get serious" about living as Christians through what they described as a "spiritual experience."

These are not primarily "knee jerk" adolescent responses. Overall, these decisions, especially those made by the older teens, were well thought out, arrived at over months and even years of consideration, and pursued because of a growing conviction that life was complicated, hazardous, and not easily navigated even with "a little help from my friends." And in fact, coming to grips with this sometimes painful reality, worked as one of the instruments of God's grace to produce an "awakening" of need that could best be addressed by responding to the message of hope they were offered.

The Message Remembered

What was the message? Or at least what part of it did the subjects find most helpful and most important? The most frequent answer offered by both groups of adolescents was "the offer of God's love, grace, and acceptance" (early = 23.6%, late = 23.3%). Early adolescents followed with "nothing particular" (18.5%) and an "assurance of heaven" (12.4%). Late adolescents likewise offered "nothing particular" (12.3%) as their second choice; but in keeping with their heightened awareness of personal need added "the possibility of knowing God" (9.2%) and "the possibility of a new life" (8.8%) as their third- and fourth-place answers.

Although another 3% to 4% of adolescents say a specific passage or image from the Bible was important, twice that many (6.7% to 8.5%) are more likely to say the "person was the message." Since 26% said that the agent's ability to explain the gospel was the most important characteristic involved in their coming to a faith decision, it is clear that the message most remembered is simply (1) "God loves you and desires a relationship with you," (2) "you can be assured of heaven" (especially for younger adolescents), (3) "you can know God personally," and (4) "you can find a new life" (especially for older adolescents). Some will note in this list little emphasis on the "bad news" of sin, guilt, and death. Actually, most adolescents don't need a lot of reminders about their "failures to hit the mark"— one of the common biblical images defining the meaning of sin. But when asked what they remember, they remember the good news that things can be different because God is on their side, not against them.

The Experience Itself

The subjects were asked how they usually referred to this time of change in their life of faith. The most commonly occurring expression used to describe the experience was "saved" (early = 30.6%, late = 23.9%). The other most frequently cited images or expressions were: "accepted Christ" (early = 18.1%, late = 15.9%), "became a Christian" (early = 13.9%, late = 12.4%), "committed myself" (early = 7.5%, late = 11.3%), and "born again" (early = 9.5%, late = 10.4%).

One of the questions simply asked if the subjects remembered their experience mostly as an emotional experience, or mostly as a time of new insight and understanding, or as an even mixture of both. The answers for adolescents and for most of the entire sample reveal an amazingly balanced bell curve. The overall percentage of persons saying their experience was primarily an "emotional" experience was 23.6%. Those saying it was primarily a matter of "insight" constituted 23.1%. Those saying it was an "even mixture" of both emotions and insight amounted to 53.4%. Adolescents scored this question: "mostly emotion" (early = 26.5%, late = 19.7%), "mostly insight" (early = 21.7%, late = 22.6%), and "an even mixture" (early = 51.7%, late = 57.7%). Most persons, including adolescents, find that coming to a "knowledge of the truth" is both an affective and a cognitive experience.

When asked what feeling or insight was most important (limiting the response to just one answer) during their time of decision or discovery, the following table summarizes the most commonly offered responses.

Table 6

Feelings and Insights Most Commonly Reported

Responses Ranked by Frequency	Early Adolescents	Late Adolescents
(1) "joy, happiness, excitement"	17.2%	15.3%
(2) "peace, contentment, relaxation"	15.4%	15.3%
(3) "relief, release, freedom"	4.0%	16.4%
(4) "acceptance, love, belonging"	11.3%	9.8%
(5) "experience of God's presence"	8.9%	8.6%
(6) "cleansed, forgiven"	6.8%	5.4%
(7) "assurance of salvation"	5.6%	4.1%
(8) "I need to surrender, obey"	4.5%	3.7%

It is clear that adolescents experience significant "refreshment" from responding to the offer of new life through trusting in Christ. The most remembered experiences and insights do not correlate in any one-to-one way with what they said they were seeking, but apparently these very real reminders of God's loving, accepting, forgiving, and freeing presence are what they needed to live their lives as committed Christians.

What Kinds of Experiences Have They Had Later in Life?

Many of us remember significant faith moments or processes in our adolescence. Some of us may have encountered skeptical parents, pastors, or peers as we tried to live out of and up to our new awareness of God's reality and what we thought this required of us. Sometimes we failed. Sometimes we ourselves became skeptical of the confidence we had placed in what we had experienced or come to believe. How common is this? What do those who acknowledge a "crystallizing process"[23] during adolescence report as the subsequent experiences and issues emerging from their faith journey as they look back from their present vantage point?

Crises of Faith

They were asked if there had been particular crises in their lives that had affected their faith negatively. Had their faith been tested? Had they ever felt that they lost their faith or abandoned commitments made during their adolescent years? Up to three answers could be recorded.

One third (34.6%) of the early adolescent group said they had experienced a time of slipping away from their faith and later returning in an act of recommitment. A slightly smaller sample (29.1%) of the late adolescent group reported this as part of their experience. When these figures are compared to the five-to-nine-year-old group (38.4%), it is clear that the earlier these decisions are made the greater the possibility of some sort of falling away. A similar number of both groups (early = 24.4%, late = 25.8%) reported experiencing times of doubt and confusion. Perhaps the only surprise in these figures is they seem, at least autobiographically speaking, somewhat low. But since it was an open-ended question and the answers were categorized only after giving the subjects a chance to name any or all experiences that had been a challenge to their faith, we may be looking at a combined total of these two answers to describe how many have experienced "seasons of doubt, confusion, and/or falling away from their faith."

To check this possibility, later editions of the survey instrument asked "Since becoming a Christian, have there been times when your faith has been severely tested or abandoned?" Over four out of five (82.8%) indicated a positive response, and even one in three of those who were still adolescents said they had been through this crisis. Apparently, some experience of "outgrowing" earlier faith experiences is quite common. The challenge is how to help more Christians realize that true faith is a living, growing, covenant relationship, and therefore requires much more than a one-time response. Perhaps another way of seeing this is to recognize that transitioning through "stages of faith," as James Fowler has called them,[24] always requires a kind of re-conversion that makes sense out of the new challenges and categories needing to be incorporated into our worldview. V. Bailey Gillespie has made a major contribution to understanding the faith of adolescents and writes in his book *The Experience of Faith*

If we really love our children and want them to grow up a faithful people, we must at some point allow freedom of choice. We cannot make our faith or beliefs theirs....

We adults often have advice to give. We have answers. We know the shortcuts. We have strong opinions wrought through difficult experience. In the name of love we often try to tell others about their faults and provide for them the information to make them better. We often have a real need to tell others something. But effective adolescent ministry indicates that we allow individuals genuine freedom....

With choice making comes the responsibility to live with the choices that have been made. This means that those of us who allow freedom must live with the choices that are not possibly our own. Fear on our part is often more real than for those making the choices. Adolescents find freedom risky, but exciting. Maturity is the result of those who allow this process to blossom....

Choosing against God is important too, because it is through wrong choices that growth occurs as well. One would not want to regularly encourage adolescents to make wrong choices, but giving respect for the choices that are made opens dialogue and moves adolescents to making decisions with a view to the responsibility involved with those decisions.[25]

All kinds of dangers crouch along the path to mature faith as a vital and informed relationship with God and a commitment to the purposes of God in our lives. Realizing that falling away and renewal are often important steps toward wholeness can be very important as we work with others who are struggling.

David was a young man of twenty-six trying to find his future in Nashville's country music industry, but he had been discovering failure was much more common than success. I met him hitchhiking along the road and offered him a ride to a job interview at an auto body shop. After discovering that I was a Methodist preacher, he told me he had been "saved" when he was twelve, but was feeling far away from the Christ he accepted those fourteen years earlier. He asked me if Methodists believed in "backsliding." I answered, "Believe in it? We practice it!" He laughed, but then said, "I've got a problem. I need to get my life right with Christ. Do you believe a guy who has really messed up and left God behind can be accepted again?" I assured him that I did, and in a quiet moment along the side of the road we talked for while and prayed. He found again the faith of his childhood, but with a much more mature understanding of its importance.

101

David asked me if I would mind going by his apartment. He told me he had a song he had written two years before and wanted me to have a copy. An hour later I submitted his song, *"That's Me Without God,"* to a Christian publication, and a few months later it appeared.

That's Me Without God

A day with no sunshine, a night with no moon
A court with no jury, a bride with no groom
A nail with no hammer, a heart with no throb
A prayer with no answer—that's me without God.

A lamp with no lighter, a train with no track
A horse with no rider, a love that won't last
A band with no leader, a door with no knob
A crop with no reaper—that's me without God.

A child with no father, a tree with no fruits
A well with no water, a plant with no roots
A school with no teacher, a ship with no dock
A church with no preacher—that's me without God.

A rose with no fragrance, a bird with no wings
A king with no treasure, a bell that won't ring
A sheep with no shepherd, a key with no lock
A man with no savior—that's me without God.
                —David Withers[26]

When persons "have tasted that the Lord is good" (1 Peter 2:3), even if they have gone away to "a distant country" (Luke 15:13-14), often they will return to the banquet, if invited. Many of us who made significant faith decisions as adolescents are awfully glad someone realized we still might need to be invited back to the table of the Lord after we had wandered some in that distant land.

Additional Faith Experiences

In addition to asking about crises in their faith journey, the subjects were asked about additional positive experiences that strengthened or confirmed their faith The table below summarizes their answers.

Table 7

Additional Faith Experiences

Additional Faith Experiences	Early Adolescents	Late Adolescents
(1) "gradual growth, nothing special"	40.4%	40.7%
(2) "baptism"	34.9%	27.3%
(3) "call to a special ministry"	28.6%	34.9%
(4) "Holy Spirit baptism or filling"	22.8%	31.2%
(5) "experience of sanctification"	15.5%	17.4%
(6) "a healing of body or spirit"	16.6%	16.0%
(7) "some other meaningful experience"	13.0%	12.4%
(8) "another conversion or restoration"	12.6%	8.4%

Although, as we have already seen, most persons feel they have gone through times when their faith was severely tested or even abandoned, only a few of those who made their primary commitment as adolescents actually report "another conversion or restoration experience." Most sense that they have had no special experiences, only gradual growth. It is interesting, however, how many indicate some sort of "call to special ministry." This does not mean a call to ordained ministry. But it does remind us that young people who are facing decisions about their purpose in life frequently believe God has something special in mind for them and that they sensed it as a call. When the sometimes overlapping expressions of "sanctification" and "Holy Spirit baptism or filling" are combined, it is easy to see that a large portion of this group has an identifiable encounter with a special work of the Holy Spirit in their lives. On the other hand, since this is central to the meaning of our faith and the promise of the new covenant, we might see the numbers as indicative of a facet of the Christian life missing in many lives.

Christian Concerns for Today

The longings and concerns of those who became Christians as adolescents are not much different from those looked at in the last chapter. Up to three concerns could be recorded for each interview. The most frequently mentioned was the desire to "grow in the Lord" (early = 39.9%, late = 41.7%). This was followed by "be a better witness" (early = 31.9%, late = 31.7%), "serve the Lord" (early = 29.5%, late = 29.3%), "have a better prayer life and personal devotions" (early = 29.9%, late = 28.9%), "know God's will" (early = 26.1%, late = 21.3%), "see a change in the Church" (early = 17.0%, late = 20.1%), "experience sanctification or be more Christlike" (early = 16.9%, late = 20.6%), and "see more justice, peace, and hope in the world" (early = 12.7%, late = 11.5%).

The Adolescent Experience of Faith

Here we have the best of times and the worst of times. The adolescent is a child becoming a man or a woman. But adolescence itself is a time in between: between the blessings and limitations of childhood and those of being an adult, between dependence and interdependence, between borrowing a faith from parents and owning a faith tried by fire, between one extreme and another. Probably in no other season of our lives after year two is there as much chemical, physiological, and personality change taking place as during this period. And it is not "straight line change."

A long list of researchers have identified adolescence as the time par excellence for conversion. William James believed this was primarily because religious conversion was above all a "unifying experience"[27] during a time of tremendous upheaval. But even such a conversion does not always succeed in holding it all together. We have found that a large majority of persons experience times of doubt, confusion, and even a willingness to abandon the "practice" of their faith though they may hold on to a slice of its profound significance. What seems to them to be true one day is false the next, and in two more days (or hours, or years) true once more. It is both a season of awakened faith and of disbelief. V. Bailey Gillespie captures this see-saw tension when he describes adolescence both as a time of developing deep personal faith and a time when "disbelief in God is frequently encountered. This rejection will become the paradox of adolescence, since it characterizes the most religious period of all. The fact is that these extremes may be encountered at different times in the same youngsters."[28]

Perhaps part of the problem lies in our inability as adults in the church to adequately represent and provide honest and profound conversations about our own faith, our own participation in the kingdom of God, our own dialogue with scripture and secular society, our own deep dependence on the whole community of faith as Christ's body, and our investment in mission and ministry. Gillespie has another good word for us in this regard.

> We must be honest with youth in our own growth. Young adults must see older adults as credible people who also have trouble with consistency and who have not sorted out all of the answers, who are not always right, victorious, or open. We are running the same race; we have not yet arrived. Let us no longer just experience religion as an abstract feeling of joy or peace but as a dynamic life-relevant mode of existence with supernatural support and personal surety in experience, all of which place the problems of living within the nurturing support of the community of belief.[29]

Probably nothing is more important in this description of the task before us than the word "community."

In an era when nuclear families are being consumed by a spirit of chaos and self destruction, it is crucial that we invest our ministry to youth with the qualities of grace, acceptance, belonging, integrity, and openness that are the fruits of the Spirit and too often missing from their experience at home or at school. We must clarify what it means to pursue "excellence" as the people of God who have found freedom through Christ to love God, love our selves, and love our neighbors. What else can overcome the skepticism and control the dropout rate of so many of our older youth?

The most frequently mentioned crisis of faith reported by those who made their conversion decisions as adolescents (early = 35.8%, late = 35.3%) was the catchall category "family, marriage, and personal relations." In addition, 29.7% of the late adolescent group reported "struggling with God's call on my life," 26.8% named "career and job decisions," 19.5% mentioned "disillusionment with other Christians" and 18.0% were impacted by "the death of a family member or close friend." Are we dealing with these and other real issues facing our teenagers? Are we even prepared to deal with these issues? If not, are we doing them a disservice, inviting young people to make "personal" decisions regarding the centrality of Christ as Lord and Savior of their lives? "Private devotions" alone simply won't cut it. Christianity is by design to be experienced and grown into as part of God's kingdom community.

Let us consider how to provoke one another to love and good deeds, not neglecting to meet together, as is the habit of some, but encouraging one another. (Hebrews 10:24-25)

The gifts he gave were that some would be apostles, some prophets, some evangelists, some pastors and teachers, to equip the saints for the work of ministry, for building up the body of Christ, until all of us come to the unity of the faith and of the knowledge of the Son of God, to maturity, to the measure of the full stature of Christ. We must no longer be children, tossed to and fro and blown about by every wind of doctrine, by people's trickery, by their craftiness in deceitful scheming. But speaking the truth in love, we must grow up in every way into him who is the head, into Christ, from whom the whole body, joined and knit together by every ligament with which it is equipped, as each part is working properly, promotes the body's growth in building itself up in love. (Ephesians 4:11-16)

The good infection requires by its very nature this kind of love and community. Otherwise, what is caught is something less than the real thing. Religion, in any form, can sometimes be the worst enemy of God's great contagion. This is what the apostle Paul learned at his conversion when he acknowledged Jesus as the Messiah and Son of God. Adolescence is the ideal time to clarify this difference and the beautiful power of godly love in a community of honest and active faith involving peers, parents, and other significant adult models.

John reminds us, "Let us love, not in word or speech, but in truth and action" (1 John 3:18). Or in the words of this ninth-century hymn—

With grateful joy and holy fear
  true charity we learn;
let us with heart and mind and strength
  now love Christ in return.
Forgive we now each other's faults
  as we our faults confess;
and let us love each other well
  in Christian holiness.
Let strife among us be unknown,
  let all contention cease;
be Christ the glory that we seek,
  be ours his holy peace.
Let us recall that in our midst
  dwells God's begotten Son;
as members of his body joined,
  we are in him made one.[30]

CHAPTER FIVE

Coming to Faith as Adults

"Every crisis means finding new bearings. The fundamental questions
have to be answered afresh: Where do you come from? Where are you
going? Who are you?"

—Jürgen Moltmann[1]

Adolescence is a time requiring tremendous adjustments, but it is
not the only time in life when special pressures arrive. The adult
years have their own fair share of rude awakenings, challenges, and
opportunities to recognize our human finitude.

The graph below, which we also examined in Chapter 3, reminds
us that females make their faith decisions earlier than males (77.1%
compared to 69.0% before the age of twenty), but it is also obvious
that after the age of twenty there is not much difference between
the genders, and there is a significantly diminished number of men
and women making initial faith decisions. Over all nearly three in
four (73.4%) confirmed they came to faith in Christ before the age
of twenty. Another 16% said their special turning point came
between the ages of twenty and twenty-nine; 6% reported a conversion in their thirties, and only 2% in the decade of their forties.
Less than 1% of the nearly four thousand interviewed reported
becoming Christians after the age of fifty.

Clearly, most who catch the good infection do so as children and
youth. But what can we say about those who "miss out" on this first
round? How do young adults, middle adults, and even a few of the "old
timers" discover they are children of God and created to be indwelt by
the Spirit of Christ? This chapter looks at the post-adolescent years and
how those who came to faith as adults describe their experience and
identify the factors most influencing their decisions and discoveries.

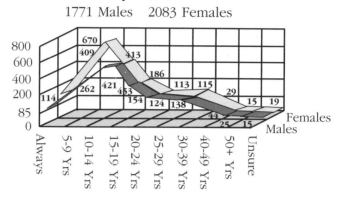

Age of Becoming a Christian by Gender
1771 Males   2083 Females

Three Adult Seasons of Faith

The data indicate that most who experience an adult conversion to Christ do so in their twenties as young adults. But a significant number of men and women throughout history and also today come to a deep personal faith experience during their thirties in what might be called their middle adult years. A much smaller number, but often persons who make significant contributions to society and to the faith of others, come to their awakening and faith decision later in life as mature adults. Often these older converts, realizing how important their new life in Christ is compared to what they had believed earlier, give themselves whole-heartedly to being bold witnesses, knowing that they have squandered too many years already to be bashful in the time they have left.

Before we look at the data and stories from contemporary adult converts who participated in the Asbury study, it might be well to set these three seasons in historical context. Persons particularly interested in stories of adult conversions would find Hugh T. Kerr and John M. Mulder's volume *Conversions* marvelously refreshing.[2] To read the personal accounts of these fifty saints of God is to recognize that the God of Abraham and Sarah is by no means only the God of children and youth. The God of all creation and all human history uses any willing vessel available, no matter the prior record or present condition. In fact, it is this message that seems to make the television series *Touched by an Angel* such an amazing success. You are never too old for God's love. It must be said, however, that it is more difficult to teach old dogs new tricks without new motivation. Here again is where an encounter with crisis, some sense of malaise, or even joyful transitions such as the birth of a child or grandchild often prompt an openness to the Holy Spirit and a new recognition that God may indeed be offering amazing grace.

A "Twentysomething" Awakened to Glory

The following conversion account is personally important to me because it is the testimony of my great-great-grandfather. It is always an amazing privilege to be invited into the life and faith story of another, but especially so when that person is part of your own story. The original is in longhand script without punctuation or standardized use of capital letters, and is at times difficult to read and decipher. With only minor editing, however, the text below is largely as it was first composed.

G.W. Crandall Born 1815 Town of Pompey County of Onondaga State of New York he lived there a year and a half he moved from there to Wales State of New York (which is called holland purchase) he lived there four years he moved from there to Ohio (moved from Ohio back to Wales) he lived there seven years

When about eight years old his mother asked him if he wouldent seek and serve the Lord he promised her he would that Spirit followed him until he was 26 years old it pressed so heavily on my mind he went to the woods about three quarters of a mile there I struggled in prayer beside of a large tree when I was there in prayer I thought I heard some one coming in the leaves I looked around and saw no one there I struggled there for a long time and went back to the house with a heavy heart   May 1841 I struggled all night in prayer next morning about sunrise God spoke peace to my troubled soul such a hallowed glory shone around my pathway that I never saw before it seemed that the birds and trees and everything was praising God

I went to one of my friends to tell him what the lord had done for me I told him we had better both start in the cause of Christ he said if nothing dident trouble him any more than that he could get along well enough I thought if he wouldent believe me I would say no more about it at the present I said no more about it

January 10th 1842 I started in Christ to let the world know that I had Christ formed within the hope of glory about sixty happy converts experienced Religion Wales Erie County New York 16th Feb 16 happy converts was Organized into the Church and baptized six weeks after 52 belonged to the Church

14th of April 1842 I and my family Emigrated for Mich arrived here

22nd here I found a little band of brethren 15 members the grace of God was with us about 10th of June 1844 I was put in as Deacon of the Freewill Baptist Church

It appears G. W. had the benefit of family faith modeling, and perhaps even some participation in church. But his own faith turning point comes years after his childhood promise to his mother. He senses the need to pursue a face-to-face encounter with God, and emerges from his night of prayer aware of a "hallowed glory." He immediately desires to bear witness to others about "Christ formed within," and his efforts are used by God to bring others to conversion. Twentysomething is a wonderful age for Christian conversion.

A "Thirtysomething" Surprised by Joy

In the last half of the twentieth century Clive Staples Lewis probably has instructed more people in the reasonableness of basic Christianity than any other writer. His rare ability to link contemporary images and storytelling with biblical truth enables nearly everyone who reads his works to come away both refreshed and informed, and some even converted. Charles Colson, converted in the aftermath of the Watergate scandal, credits the witness of his friend Tom Phillips and a copy of Lewis's *Mere Christianity* as the torpedo that hit him amidships. "That one chapter ripped through the protective armor in which I had unknowingly encased myself for forty-two years. Of course I had not known God. *How could I?* I had been concerned with myself.... I saw myself as never before. And the picture was ugly."[3]

But this story is Lewis's own story, which he labeled *Surprised by Joy* in his spiritual autobiography. A devout atheist, a scholar of renowned teaching at Magdalen College, Oxford University, and a man of principle, C. S. Lewis was one of the least likely thirty-one-year-old converts imaginable. But these are the "surprises" of God.

Remember, I had always wanted, above all things, not to be "interfered with." I had wanted (mad wish) "to call my soul my own." I had been far more anxious to avoid suffering than to achieve delight. I had always aimed at limited liabilities. The supernatural itself had been to me, first, an illicit dram, and then, as by a drunkard's reaction, nauseous....

You must picture me alone in that room in Magdalen, night after night, feeling, whenever my mind lifted even for a second from my work, the steady, unrelenting approach of Him whom I so earnestly desired not to meet. That which I greatly feared had at last come upon me. In the Trinity Term of 1929, I gave in, and admitted that God was God, and knelt and prayed: perhaps, that night, the most dejected and reluctant convert in all England. . . .

It must be understood that the conversion . . . was only to Theism, pure and simple, not to Christianity. I knew nothing yet about the Incarnation. . . .

I know very well when, but hardly how, that final step was taken. I was driven to Whipsnade one sunny morning. When we set out I did not believe that Jesus Christ is the Son of God, and when we reached the zoo I did. Yet I had not exactly spent the journey in thought. Nor in great emotion. . . . It was more like when a man, after long sleep, still lying motionless in bed, becomes aware that he is now awake.[4]

The one who first referred to the work of the Holy Trinity in us as "the good infection" and in so doing partially inspired this book, actually caught the contagion on his way to the zoo while riding in the sidecar of a motorcycle driven by his brother.

A "Fortysomething" Loved to New Life

Nancy Marsh Griffin seemed caught in a horrible whirlpool of anger, argument, and death. When Nancy was fourteen her mother died during the night, just hours after a quarrel had erupted between them. Nancy's first husband, a pilot, was killed when his plane crashed three days after a stormy argument chased him from the house. Her second husband drank himself to death in a house filled with strife. Her five daughters, constantly bobbing up and down in this tempest, had their own share of social and emotional battles, and only by the grace of God, literally, survived.

Susan was the oldest, and from Nancy's perspective had suffered the most. Dread filled this mother's heart when Susan, now in college at Boston, called to say she was coming home for the weekend.

I pictured another tense confrontation. That was the way it always was when she was home, bossing her younger sisters, criticizing, venting her hostility. . . .

When she arrived, though, the pretty, blond young woman who stood in the doorway as I hugged her was not the stony daughter I had known. She smiled, and her eyes brightened, and I knew there was something different about her.

"Mom," she said, "something wonderful has happened! I'm a Christian."

I laughed, thinking she was joking. "Of course you're a Christian, Susan," I said. Hadn't I made certain my girls were baptized and got a Christian education?

"Sure, Mom, but this is different." She then told me how some friends at school had told her that Jesus Christ could make a difference in her life. . . . One day in the dorm she decided to go along with them when they went to their room to pray.

"It was beautiful, Mom," she said. "I just asked Christ to come into my life and straighten things out. And He did."

Nancy was happy for her daughter's newfound peace and the change in her spirit, but she felt she had damaged too many lives for God to ever forgive her.

Susan returned to college but began to regularly call home to chat with and cheer her mother. Often she would tell of new things she was learning about herself and her faith, even reading Bible passages to her mother over the phone. Finally, in desperation, one day Nancy blurted out to her, "How can I understand what you're saying if I don't even have a Bible to read?" A few days later a package arrived, a Bible, from Susan, with an inscription on the first page quoting John 14:16, 18-20.

At the end of the quote, Susan had also penned, "I thank God for giving me such a wonderful mother, one who cared for me and loved me. May we always be together in Christ."

I clutched the Bible, and my eyes lingered over Susan's words. Suddenly I opened my mouth and whispered, "Forgive me, Lord." It was as if a gash had been sliced into my wall of fear and guilt, and I felt my spirit lift. *Someone* was taking the burden out of my heart. I was being forgiven. I could feel the peace. . . . Now I knew exactly what Susan had meant when she said, "I'm a Christian." And I knew just what a difference it makes.[5]

Three Generations and Some Differences

A great deal has been written during the last decade about generational differences, especially comparing the "Builders," "Boomers," and "Busters." Actually, many writers prefer to divide this tidy three-part distinction of today's generations into five, or ten, or even more.[6] William Strauss and Neil Howe in their influential text *Generations: The History of America's Future, 1584 to 2069,* define a generation as "a cohort group whose length approximates the span of a phase of life and whose boundaries are fixed by peer personality."[7] Without getting lost in sociological details, what is being described is a shared heritage of experience based on the most significant societal events, values, and characteristics. For example, one of the "defining moments" for "Builders" (born before 1946) might be the bombing of Pearl Harbor. "Boomers" (born 1946–1964) have no way of connecting to the significance of that event, but do remember where they were when they heard "President Kennedy has been shot." "Busters" (born 1965–1983) only know that dark day in Dallas by hearsay and television; but they remember the *Challenger* disaster or the dismantling of the Berlin Wall.

Little is made of these generational distinctives in relation to the primary theme of this book. Our focus is more the phase of life rather than the generation. Nevertheless, some interesting variations based on the three generations are worth noting. For example, in the table below note the differences in which agent of Christian witness proved most important to each generation.

Table 8

Generations by Primary Agents of Influence

Generation	Mother	Pastor	Friend or Peer	Youth Leader
Builders	16.7%	11.4%	6.2%	1.1%
Boomers	9.2%	10.4%	14.9%	5.0%
Busters	8.2%	6.6%	13.4%	10.6%

A similar pattern exists when examining which persons proved most helpful in actually helping the converts come to a faith decision.

Table 9

Generations by Agents of Christian Decision

Generation	Pastor	Evangelist	Friend or Peer	Youth Leader
Builders	21.0%	12.5%	4.9%	2.0%
Boomers	17.9%	11.4%	12.4%	4.9%
Busters	12.4%	8.6%	10.2%	11.6%

113

Pastors and parents have not been as effective as agents of Christian witness and conversion for young adults in the Buster generation as they were in previous generations. This generation has more likely been influenced and won to faith by friends and youth leaders. It is not surprising, therefore, that the physical settings they were in when they made their decisions differ significantly from other generations.

Table 10

Generations by Decision Location

Generation	Own Church	Own Home	Camp or Retreat
Builders	50.8%	15.4%	7.0%
Boomers	33.7%	20.5%	11.4%
Busters	28.9%	23.7%	18.9%

Because of the obvious changes in the importance of friends and youth leaders in bringing today's new adults to faith, it is not surprising that the social environments have also shifted.

Table 11

Generations by Social Context

Generation	Special Church Service	Regular Church Service	Alone	A Small Group	One Other Person
Builders	30.9%	26.1%	15.9%	11.6%	8.2%
Boomers	22.6%	20.9%	24.1%	14.2%	11.9%
Busters	19.3%	15.7%	21.4%	16.3%	20.5%

The same could be said for the expressions we prefer to use when describing our encounters with God. Although most of the subjects in all three generations preferred to describe their experience as when they were "saved," other expressions frequently cited were "accepted Christ," "became a Christian," and "born again" (10.5%). As can be seen in the table below, "Busters" were more likely to talk about when they "accepted Christ" and "Builders" were more likely to describe their experience as "born again" than were the other two generations.

Table 12

Generations by Preferred Expression

Generation	Saved	Accepted Christ	Became a Christian	Born Again	Made a Commitment
Builders	30.1%	12.6%	7.5%	12.2%	8.2%
Boomers	26.0%	16.3%	12.4%	10.7%	11.9%
Busters	28.5%	18.0%	12.6%	8.8%	20.5%

No doubt several possible implications and applications could be proposed on the basis of these statistics, but in general it should be noted that fewer and fewer persons have been brought to faith in Christ through decisions made in regular or special church services. Is this a change in the opportunities presented in such settings? Are many pastors less evangelistic? Probably. But it is also likely due to cultural changes and social mobility that Boomers and Busters have been more comfortable participating in interactive conversations with peers regarding matters of faith than were their parents or grandparents. Boomers and Busters more likely have had youth groups and retreats to attend and friends discussing "religion" with them in their homes. The data do not allow a cause and effect relationship to be proposed, but they do indicate a clear shift in some "who," "when," and "where" issues we will need to consider in the next chapter aimed at asking how will we best serve as Christ's ambassadors for the coming generations.

Who Are the Contagious Influences?

In keeping with the primary thrust of this chapter, we return to asking how adults come to faith based on their age or stage of life rather than their generation. As noted in Chapter 4, persons making personal commitments to Christ as adults (as compared to those doing so as children and adolescents) are likely to have had reduced positive church exposure and faith modeling when they were children. So who are the "carriers" for those making decisions as adults? As might be expected, the answers vary some by the stage of adult life being examined.

Agents Who Create the Desire for Personal Faith

The 942 in the Asbury study who became Christians as adults between the ages of twenty and forty-nine reported that their interest in a personal faith encounter with God was most likely stimulated by friends. There is a natural shift taking place away from parents as persons of influence, and an interesting increase in the influence of other relatives, a spouse, and to some degree the pastor.

Table 13

Age Christian Compared to Persons of Influence

Age of Becoming Christian	Friend or Peer	Spouse	Other Relative	Pastor
20-24	24.5%	5.9%	11.4%	10.9%
25-29	18.5%	9.7%	12.2%	8.4%
30-39	18.1%	12.2%	10.2%	12.2%
40-49	13.5%	16.2%	13.5%	12.2%

In a similar study done in England by John Finney the "other family members" were identified as their own children, grandparents, brothers, and sisters.[8] In a study conducted by James Wesley Griffin in postcommunist Estonia, brothers and sisters were identified separately, and still 13.2% were listed as "other relative."[9] Griffin's study is also very instructive in noting "friends" were most important as agents of influence, and that sometimes the "persons of influence" were actually a group—most likely "a worshipping congregation"

(26.1%), a "youth group" (including young adults 17.6%), or a "home fellowship group" (16.0%). Experiencing Christian community is always important in helping persons catch the good infection, but without a "friend" to invite and encourage attendance, few make their way into the fellowship of new life. John Finney affirms the importance of the group in the faith journeys of the more than five hundred subjects participating in the British study.

> We asked participants if they regarded one special person as particularly influential or whether it was a group of people. Only about a quarter looked to one person as the key influence though, of course, there may have been one person who had been particularly helpful, or who introduced them to the group. *For most people the corporate life of the church is a vital element in the process of becoming a Christian and for about a quarter it is the vital factor.* Forms of evangelism which fail to recognize this are doomed.[10]

Although our primary purpose is to look at the persons having the most influence, it is also important to note some having the least. The adult converts in the Asbury study confirm that "strangers" account for only 1.4%, "fathers" for 1.9%, "evangelists" 2.9%, "neighbors" 3.5%, "mothers" 6.2%, and "God alone" (no other remembered human agent) is mentioned as most influential in 11.3% of these cases. The older we get the more likely we are to be impacted by the witness of a trusted close friend, or a family member other than a parent.

When asked what it was about these agents of influence that most caught their attention and made them interested in examining the Christian life, they responded quite similarly to those who came to faith as adolescents. The most important characteristic was their "obvious relationship with God" (37.4%). In second place was something particularly attractive about their personality or character (21.7%). Closely following in third place was the special care shown by the witnesses to the subjects (18.6%). Interestingly enough, the answers were almost identical across the adult age groups except for this third quality. The twenty- to twenty-four-year-old converts rated it only at 17.5% while the forty to forty-nine group valued it as the most important quality 27% of the time, and those becoming Christians between the ages of fifty to fifty-nine rated it highest of all qualities at 36.0%. This shift of influence from one who obviously "loves God" to one who "cares for me" may be particularly important as we consider how to best communicate God's love to older adults with more of a "show me" mentality.

Agents Who Help Adults Make Decisions

Much like the examples cited earlier in this chapter, the most common person mentioned as the agent of decision was "God alone" (21.2%). This figure reached a full 25% for young adults in their late twenties, and overall is very much in line with the Estonian study (20.9%). Almost all persons who make faith decisions as adults seem to be prepared for their encounter with God by the witness of others and a variety of sensitizing experiences and insights. However, when it comes time to cross the line from curiosity to commitment nearly a quarter of these persons find themselves alone with God in their own homes, in their automobiles, in their own churches, or on a spiritual retreat.

Almost as many (19.3%) indicate that a "pastor" helped them arrive at their faith decision. This percentage increases from about 15% for those making faith decisions in their twenties to nearly 35% for those in their forties. Quite naturally a high percentage of these persons (61.4%) indicate that they were in their own churches when they opened themselves to God's gift of new life through faith in Christ. Another 11.7% were in their own homes when their pastor helped them experience Christian conversion, and 7.3% indicated they were on retreat.

"Friends" are the third most common agents of decision for adult converts at 16.3%. Most who recall a friend leading them to Christ remember it taking place in their own home (24.9%). Other locations included: "my church" (14.1%), "on retreat" (12.9%), "another church" (12.6%), and "in another home" (12.3%). With friends, almost any place will do; any place that is, that the friend is.

The qualities of these "faith friends" which made them most helpful as spiritual guides include: (1) "their relationship with God" (29.0%), (2) "their explanation of the biblical message" (23.7%), (3) "how they cared for me" (18.1%), and (4) "their character and personality" (14.3%). No significant variation on these priorities appeared when the generations "Builders," "Boomers," and "Busters" were considered separately. Transparent spiritual integrity, or how well the "light shines forth" from our own relationship with God is paramount. But close behind is our ability to clarify for others the biblical message of hope offered to all who will come to Christ.

What Kinds of Experiences Did They Have?

It's time to hear from some of those who were willing to share how they caught the good infection as adults.

Rod

Rod was the consummate southern businessman—disarmingly hospitable, yet very much in control, wearing a mask and keeping the veneer of his life well-ordered and polished. He began his sharing with a light-hearted, matter-of-fact description of his childhood. But then his mood shifted as he described the pain. His was a home without the benefit of any church influence, and one where abuse and abandonment were hidden by opulence. When he went on to describe his actual conversion experience the veneer cracked open as he graphically recounted his emotionally charged encounter with something he did not at the time understand. He recalled being overcome with guilt and shame, and crying uncontrollably without knowing why. He describes this experience now as "the time Jesus dumped on me."

A friend referred him to a minister who interpreted the mysterious event that awakened his soul, and who clarified the gospel while showing personal concern for him. The minister was both the agent of influence (after the experience of facing his own emptiness prompted by the Holy Spirit) and the agent of helping Rod come to a decision of accepting God's forgiveness, grace, love, and power to live a new life through Christ. He was transparent about his struggles and doubts, his backsliding and failures; but was always encouraged in his pilgrimage as a Christian by dear friends in a men's Bible study and by a special "dream" or "vision" which he sensed came from God to assure him of God's provision for every need. He knew he did not know all the "right answers," but he was sure of God's love and that his heart had been changed.

Dorothy

Dorothy did not grow up in a family active in church or openly willing to acknowledge faith in God. Her parents "made no pretenses," Dorothy explained; there were "no blood relatives, no friends, no peers, nobody" to help her find her way spiritually and grow in faith "*except* my godmother!" she recounted. She had been baptized as an infant in the Roman Catholic Church. Her godmother took it seriously as God's mark on little Dorothy even if no one else did. From as long back as she could now remember her godmother focused her life on God and the Church and on what it meant to live out a life of Christian witness caring for others. Obedience, obligation, and observance seemed to be the formula emphasized by her godmother, the nuns, and the priests for living a Christian life. She never questioned it, though she does recall longing for something more.

She always thought of herself as a Christian, and remembered her confirmation and first communion experiences as important milestones. But as a young adult she fell in love and married a man who was Methodist, not Catholic. Over the course of several years they attended both churches as well as an Episcopal congregation, trying to find what would be the one faith for their entire family. Finally, they settled on being Methodists. Dorothy insisted she be (re-)baptized before she joined, and thinks of this as a fresh start. Both she and her husband became quite active in church in such areas as worship attendance, committees, offices, and other responsibilities. But the old feeling that there most be something more returned.

Then one day a friend named Gina, whose life seemed to just bubble over with a joy in everything she did, asked Dorothy and her husband if they would like to attend a special retreat weekend called Tres Dias (Three Days) which was designed to help people walk closer to Christ. They both agreed. Gina says, "To say that the weekend was a life-changing experience would be an understatement. It was here that my husband really met Jesus for the first time. I discovered a new depth in my relationship with the Lord, and now knew that our love affair was mutual. It was finally real!"

Calvin

At the time he was interviewed, Calvin was in prison serving a five-year sentence—not his first. Calvin said he had no real exposure to Christianity as a child or a youth. Even though the family he was raised in considered themselves Baptists, they never attended church or talked about their faith. In fact, when asked who influenced his interest in becoming a Christian, he could name no one.

He said his interest began when he was thirty. Passed out from a drug overdose, he had a vision in which God told him "Go to church." He became obedient to the vision and began attending a local Baptist church on a regular basis. He found his way out of drugs, was baptized, and became a member of the church. In time he became involved in home Bible studies where he was discipled by mature Christians, and was even elected and installed as a deacon.

Yet he thinks of his true conversion coming at thirty-nine while in a jail cell. He had fallen back into his old habits, and was arrested and convicted on drug charges. He lost his car dealership, his standing in the community, and his reputation in church. There was no vision this time, just a truly contrite heart turning to God. He remembered "I felt an immediate peace and was assured that everything was going to work out." The scripture that came to his mind was Luke 4:18:

> The Spirit of the Lord is upon me,
>   because he has anointed me
>   to bring good news to the poor.
> He has sent me to proclaim release to the captives
>   and recovery of sight to the blind,
>   to let the oppressed go free

He knew he "was found" and that God was calling him to a true and deep commitment of his life and to serve others.

Julia

Julia grew up in a farming community and regularly attended with her family the Methodist church in town. Church was important in the life of her family and in the life of the whole community. Yet she could not recall anyone ever talking about a personal relationship with Jesus Christ. There were two persons, a Sunday school teacher and a piano teacher, who impressed her as a child with their genuine Christian faith; but as far as she could recall, nothing was ever articulated about how such a faith becomes real for others.

The church provided the context for her marriage and for raising her family. She and her children participated in church activities both at the local and the judicatory level. Caring for neighbors and serving in the community were just a way of life. She also enjoyed a community Bible study group.

But her comfort zone was about to be challenged. A new pastor was appointed to her church, and began talking and preaching about knowing Christ in a personal way. She heard that God was personally interested in her and looking for a deep fellowship to exist between them. This "new message" created a longing in her life to know God more fully. One Monday, at home by herself, as she mulled over the "personal gospel" emphasis from the Sunday sermon, she quietly surrendered herself to Christ and felt "a deep sense of relief," a clearing of her mind, and a whole new meaning in things she had already known and done for years. She refers to this moment as the time when she was "found by Christ." Her greatest desire was for her family to come to know Christ in a personal way and not just be "caught up in the forms of faith." Her deepest regret was that she had not known this reality earlier in order to better encourage and equip her children for living life the way it was meant to be.

Patterns from the Data

There are a multitude of stories; each one different, unique, and powerful in its own way, and wonderfully encouraging to those of us who hear again and again how willing God is to meet us just as we are. Yet, as unique as each story is, some patterns emerge from the nearly one thousand stories condensed into computer data. Data are never as exciting as stories. But it is difficult to learn some things from stories where the emphasis often seems to be on God's ability to address each of us through our own unique frame of reference and context. The wise men made it to Bethlehem by following their astrological insights and obeying a strange star. Mary and Joseph made it because of a tax decree from an occupying, foreign government. The shepherds made it because angels appeared and filled the night sky with the glory of song. How do *we* get to "Bethlehem?" God's way, and Christ will lead us, if we will follow.

What Were You Seeking?

The table below shows that not all persons today are following the same path to transforming faith. When given a chance to describe any particular kind of fulfillment they were seeking when they came to faith, some interesting patterns emerge based on their ages.

Table 14

Age Christian Compared to Fulfillment Sought

Age of Becoming Christian	Fill a Void Peace	Relationship with God	Meaning Purpose	Better Life Help	Salvation from Sin
20-29	22.7%	18.1%	13.7%	9.6%	10.3%
30-39	34.5%	12.2%	9.0%	11.0%	8.2%
40-49	27.0%	20.3%	6.8%	10.8%	10.8%

The greatest need acknowledged by all of the adults when they came to Christ, was the need to fill an emptiness, a void, a "God-shaped vacuum" that nothing else in life had thus far been able to fill. This longing seems most acute in those who came to their faith discoveries during their "thirtysomething" years. Second in line was a specific desire to find a personal "relationship with God." Third place varied by age group. "Twentysomethings" were more desirous of "meaning and purpose," while "thirtysomethings" wanted a "better life and help for living," and "fortysomethings" split evenly between "a better life" and "salvation from sin." Being aware of these patterns as we listen to the longings of adult "seekers" could help us better hear the Holy Spirit's guidance when offering words of wisdom and witness.

Were You Aware in Any Way of God's Leading?

Among the 942 subjects converted as adults, 5.6% said they remembered no special sense of being led by God to their new decisions. Most frequently they reported "a growing conviction" of needing to do something about their faith (twenties = 33.5%, thirties = 28.2%, forties = 24.3%). Following close behind in second place they "faced a crisis" of some kind which forced them to acknowledge their need for God (twenties = 17.0%, thirties = 20.4%, forties = 25.7%). Third and fourth positions showed little variation between the age groups and were respectively "a growing hunger for God" (10.8%) and "just a gradual quest on my part" (10.4%). Other ways they reported experiencing God's leading were through: "a special spiritual experience" (8.4%), "something I read or heard someone say" (6.9%), and "the influence of my family" (3.0%). Five percent offered a variety of other ways through which they had sensed God's guidance prior to their moments of turnaround.

It must be remembered that these persons are looking back to a time in their lives which may have transpired ten, twenty, or thirty years earlier. Our memories are not perfect. Nevertheless, as many of these Christian men and women recalled the work of God that brought them to new commitments and new depths of faith in Christ, they were deeply touched. Most had not talked about these things with anyone before, or at least not for years. Those who conducted the interviews often reported that listening to their subjects recall their stories seemed to be "sacred moments" full of power and a shared humility before the majesty and grace of God.

What Part of the Message Shared Most Influenced Your Decision?

Those making faith decisions as children or youth often answered (children = 20.5%, youth = 15.8%) they could not remember anything particular about the message. Only 8.3% of the adult converts gave this answer. Most frequently they remembered a message telling them of "God's love, grace, and acceptance" (twenties = 22.4%, thirties = 25.3%, forties = 35.1%). Other emphases remembered were: "the possibility of a new life" (12.4%), "the person *was* the message" (9.4%), "the possibility of knowing God/Jesus" (8.7%), and the "assurance of heaven or salvation" (6.8%).

One problem with reducing any large number of personal stories into neat categories is that the nuances are lost. Seldom did the subjects answer questions like this one using a five- or six-word sentence nicely fitting into a tidy box on the response form. If you were asked this question, more than likely several ideas would come to mind as you tried to recover from your dusty memories what *most* influenced your response to the gospel offered, if you could remember at all. The subjects worked hard to get back in touch with these "sleeping memories." The general categories offered here are just that, "general." As such, they lose much of their sharpness, specificity, and uniqueness. Indeed, they become "flat" pictures, caricatures, as opposed to their original full 3-D reality. But recognizing patterns in life, even in the face of enormous diversity, is what makes life manageable. If as we try to share the message of God's saving and transforming love in Jesus, we recognize the uniqueness of each person as well as the challenges we share in common, we stand a better chance of "connecting" the gospel's universal truth with each person's and each group's deepest needs.

What Do You Remember About the Experience Itself?

We already noted earlier in this chapter that some patterns change according to our generational identity. The persons involved as evangelistic agents have shifted through the years, as have the locations and social contexts for our faith decisions and the language used to describe the conversion experiences we have. Most adult converts, like the children and youth, remember their experience as being an even mixture of new insight and deeply felt emotions (53.9%); and as we have seen before, about a quarter remembered the experience as mostly new insight (24.6%) and nearly as many (21.5%) say it was mostly emotional.

The particular insights and emotions they report are seen in the table below.

Table 15

Feelings and Insights Most Commonly Reported

Overall Responses Ranked by Frequency	Ages 20-29	Ages 30-39	Ages 40-49
(1) "peace, contentment, relaxation"	17.0%	20.0%	15.1%
(2) "relief, release, freedom"	17.5%	15.3%	16.4%
(3) "joy, happiness, excitement"	10.8%	13.7%	9.6%
(4) "acceptance, love, belonging"	10.6%	7.1%	13.7%
(5) "experience of God's presence"	9.5%	4.7%	5.5%
(6) "cleansed, forgiven"	6.7%	4.7%	11.0%
(7) "God and gospel are real"	4.4%	4.3%	2.7%
(8) "assurance of salvation"	3.9%	4.3%	4.1%

Perhaps the only figure that stands out is the ranking of "acceptance, love, belonging" for the forty- to forty-nine-year-old converts. Normally, this is seen as a developmental need earlier in life, an adolescent and early young adult issue. Perhaps as we can see from some of the testimonies cited above, older adult converts—perhaps especially men[11]—have missed this earlier in life and are finally catching up as they experience God's amazing, unconditional love.

Such is the story my own father might tell. An only child raised in a somewhat cold, adult world, fashioned by gifts and training to be a "do it right" electrical engineer, he was fifty-three when a heart attack almost ended his life. In the months of healing that followed, he was surrounded by a band of faithful friends who themselves were discovering new life in their relationship with Jesus and the Holy Spirit. When Vic's "breakthrough" came, he was overwhelmed with a sense of love beyond measure. As a member of the "Builder" generation and an engineer, he had lived his whole life trying to "do it right" and "figure" everything out. One night in a small group prayer and sharing meeting, he suddenly realized that God's gift of the Spirit and the abundant life in Jesus was just that, a gift! He couldn't grasp it or own it by logic alone as though it were some cosmic answer to an algebraic formula. So he simply opened himself to the Gift, received the Gift, and a dam broke. All he could do for hours was cry, and laugh, and praise God!

What Follows as They Try to Walk in Faith?

Previously we have seen that those who come to faith as children and adolescents frequently have a difficult time "holding on" for the long haul. Many go through seasons of doubt and confusion, falling away or "backsliding" as some have called it. What happens with those who come to their faith as adults? What crises of faith do they encounter? What additional faith experiences to they report? What are their deepest longings for themselves and others?

Crises of Faith Following Conversion

When adult converts were asked "What significant crises of faith have you faced?" they openly acknowledged that all had not been

126

smooth and easy for them. They had to learn to make the adjustments to daily living that their new faith and relationship with God required. Sometimes they failed, sometimes they fumbled, sometimes they found themselves struggling with old habits as they were learning how to develop new ones. But as might be expected, their answers were not identical to those cited by our younger disciples. The table below reveals the difficulties most frequently mentioned by adult converts.

Table 16

Crises of Faith Most Commonly Reported

Responses Ranked by Overall Adult Frequency	Ages 20-29	Ages 30-39	Ages 40-49
(1) "marriage, family, relationships"	39.4%	36.4%	33.8%
(2) "career and job decisions"	33.4%	29.1%	33.8%
(3) "God's call on my life"	29.2%	25.6%	27.0%
(4) "disillusionment with Christians"	19.7%	27.5%	21.6%
(5) "doubt and confusion"	21.3%	20.2%	25.7%
(6) "backsliding"	22.3%	14.7%	10.8%
(7) "death of friend/family member"	16.0%	16.7%	13.5%

Among those who came to faith as children between the ages of five and nine, 38.4% said they had experienced backsliding and a time of recommitment. Youth converts cited this experience less frequently (ten to fourteen = 34.5%, fifteen to nineteen = 29.1%), and it is clear from the chart above that this crisis becomes less of a problem as the age of coming to faith increases. No significant variation in the other crises faced shows up by age of faith decision except in the categories of "career and job decision" (affects more adult converts) and "death of a friend or family member" (affects more child converts). It is interesting to note, then, that "family and relationship" problems top the list for crises faced that challenge our faith. Knowing this should better arm us to fight this faith-consuming dragon with positive and honest preaching, teaching, prayer, and Christian presence during times

127

when others are struggling and hurting. Probably the same could be said for each of these challenges.

Additional Faith Experiences Following Conversion

In our study, when persons told their stories of faith and were asked "What significant additional faith experiences have you had?" they most often responded (38.9%), "Nothing special or extra, just gradual growth." This response was as high as 48% for those who said they were always Christians, and as low as 32% for those converted between ages twenty-five and twenty-nine. Busters were more likely to report "nothing special" than were the Builders or Boomers, which is understandable since they are the youngest generation.

The most frequently remembered "special faith event" other than conversion was "water baptism" (31.3% overall and most reported by the forty- to forty-nine-year-old converts—43.2%). In second place and continuing a trend noticed previously, adult converts interviewed for the Asbury study reported the additional faith experience of "sensing a special call to ministry" (twenty to twenty-nine = 31.5%, thirty to thirty-nine = 28.7%, forty to forty-nine = 24.3%).[12] The third most common response noted in recent interviews, at least among Boomers, was "the birth of a child."

But considering the theme of God's glorious infection, the most interesting responses given by the adult converts were two kinds of special encounters with the Holy Spirit—"sanctification" and "the baptism or filling of the Holy Spirit." William James in his *Varieties of Religious Experience* lectures in 1901 and 1902 devoted two lectures to conversion and three to "saintliness," which he describes as "the ripe fruits of religion."[13] He finds the account of Jonathan Edwards one of the most helpful descriptions of this "condition."

> Last night was the sweetest night I ever had in my life.... All night I continued in a constant, clear, and lively sense of the heavenly sweetness of Christ's excellent love, of his nearness to me, and of my dearness to him.... As I awoke the next morning, it seemed to me that I had entirely done with myself. I felt that the opinions of the world concerning me were nothing, and that I had no more to do with any outward interest of my own than with that of a person whom I never saw. The glory of God seemed to swallow up every wish and desire of my heart.[14]

Some traditions believe that such "saintly," "holy," or "sanctified"[15] experiences of transformation brought by the Holy Spirit are reserved for a small minority of souls. In other traditions, however, sanctification—saintliness—holiness is the expected outcome for every Christian who has caught the good infection. Historically this has been a special emphasis of the Wesleyan or Methodist movement. John Wesley taught that all who trusted Christ for forgiveness of sins should also expect to be liberated from the bondage of sin's habits and be fully empowered by the Holy Spirit to love God with all their heart, and their neighbor as themselves. This second work of grace, often coming in an instant and usually several months or even years after "initial salvation," Wesley described as "full salvation," "Christian perfection," "scriptural holiness," or "entire sanctification."

In eighteenth-century England perhaps as many as 15% or more of the Methodists claimed such a work of grace in their lives.[16] In our sample, the overall figures are actually quite similar, although no attempt was made to insure that those claiming the experience today would meet Wesley's standards.

When the sometimes overlapping experiences of "sanctification" and "baptized or filled with the Holy Spirit" are compared by age of conversion, generation, and present denomination, quite an interesting pattern emerges. The three tables below make it easier to see the larger picture.

Table 17

Transforming Encounters with the Holy Spirit by Age Christian

Age of Becoming a Christian	"Sanctification"	Baptism/Filling by Holy Spirit
Always	9.0%	18.5%
5-9	19.0%	26.6%
10-14	15.5%	22.8%
15-19	17.4%	31.2%
20-24	19.4%	32.8%
25-29	12.1%	34.7%
30-39	10.1%	35.7%
40-49	10.8%	20.3%

Table 18

Transforming Encounters with the Holy Spirit by Generation

Generation	"Sanctification"	Baptism/Filling by Holy Spirit
Builders	19.4%	23.3%
Boomers	15.6%	31.8%
Busters	12.9%	22.7%

Table 19

Transforming Encounters with the Holy Spirit by Denomination

Present Denomination	"Sanctification"	Baptism/Filling by Holy Spirit	Combined Total
United Methodist	15.6%	30.0%	45.6
Free Methodist	23.3%	18.7%	42.0
Wesleyan	43.6%	11.7%	53.3
Nazarene	48.7%	25.6%	74.3
Salvation Army	22.2%	19.4%	41.6
CMA (Alliance)	17.2%	17.2%	34.4
Baptist	6.5%	15.5%	22.0
Presbyterian	9.9%	17.3%	27.2
Lutheran	5.7%	31.4%	37.1
Roman Catholic	1.9%	7.7%	9.6
Pentecostal	5.4%	74.7%	80.1
None	14.5%	32.7%	47.2
Other	9.7%	26.5%	36.2

Although there may be other ways of describing this significant Christian experience with the Holy Spirit, and although some may link it to their initial acceptance of Christ rather than acknowledge it as a separate experience, the clear thesis of this book is that the contagious God who is Holy Trinity provides all we need to move on from "one degree of glory to another" (2 Corinthians 3:18). This moving on "in order that we may share his holiness" (Hebrews 12:10) is dependent on becoming more aware of and surrendered to God's all-embracing love poured into us and through us by the Holy Spirit (John 7:38-39; Romans 5:1-5). If such refining encounters with this contagious Spirit are a key ingredient for fulfilling God's design for us as Christ's church, we might do well in light of the indicators above to examine the degree to which we are encouraging today's ministers and church members to seek and pray for this "true religion" as Wesley called it.

Greatest Concerns for Today

Generally the three adult groups agree on most of their larger concerns for their own lives, their churches, and the world. Most frequently mentioned by all is the desire to grow in their faith and their relationship with God. Those converted later in life seem more likely to want to make a difference in this world. They more frequently mention a desire to be better witnesses, to serve God with their lives, to know God's will, and to see more justice, peace, and hope in the world. They are less likely to prioritize their devotional life and sanctification, but equally as concerned as the others to see certain changes come to their churches.

Table 20

Concerns Most Commonly Reported

Responses Ranked by Overall Adult Frequency	Ages 20-29	Ages 30-39	Ages 40-49
(1) "to grow in the Lord"	42.2%	42.4%	43.2%
(2) "to serve God with my life"	35.9%	29.6%	40.5%
(3) "be a better witness to others"	33.4%	33.1%	43.2%
(4) "to know God's will"	21.6%	28.8%	31.1%
(5) "better devotional & prayer life	24.6%	19.1%	8.1%

(6) "sanctification/Christlikeness"	17.9%	16.3%	12.2%
(7) "change in the Church"	16.3%	19.1%	17.6%
(8) "justice, peace, hope for world"	11.3%	10.5%	17.6%

A couple of interesting differences show up between the generations. The Boomers (31.6%) and Busters (27.8%) are more interested in learning how to have better devotions and pray than are the Builders (16.7%). This may be because the older Builder generation is already satisfied with their level of personal devotions and prayer, or because they are from a generation that was composed more of "Marthas" than "Marys." A second generational difference is a bit surprising in light of all the talk about older persons being resistant to change in the church. Builders (22.7%) led the pack in expressing a desire for a change in the church. Boomers followed with 18.6% and Busters communicated this concern only 13.5% of the time. Although the survey did not tabulate the nature of the changes they were interested in, it is encouraging to see even this kind of interest among some older adults in our churches.

Perhaps most rewarding, at least to this writer, is the high level of interest expressed in being better witnesses, especially among the Builder generation. It is for these persons in all generations that this book is written. In the next and final chapter the lessons most obvious from the thousands of stories of faith we have examined will be compiled in a "Carriers' Guidebook." But first, one more story to show how God works first to bring us to faith in Christ, and then to send us as contagious witnesses for others.

Finally, at Fifty

The interview began in Louisville, Kentucky, with Neil sharing his great love for baseball and the San Francisco Giants. He had been especially touched by the story of Dave Dravecky who following the amputation of his pitching arm and the loss of his baseball career, wrote two books telling how Jesus Christ had carried him through. These testimonies of trusting in Jesus would not always have "blessed" Neil.

He was born in New Jersey into a traditional, conservative Jewish family. He described his mother as "a loving but very strong Jewish mother, a true servant who loved being involved at temple." His father, a successful businessman, was more passive about his faith, but attended temple most Friday evening services and on high holy days. Though part of a conservative congregation, Neil recalled that his rabbi was "very young and very orthodox."

As his father's business grew more and more successful, the family moved from the city to the suburbs into an "all-white, all-Christian" neighborhood. "I was the only Jew," he said wistfully, "an oddity." As a youth, Neil was a great athlete. This helped him find acceptance in the "good times," but in the bad times, "I was the stupid Jew boy!" The family continued to attend temple, but it was now far removed from their neighborhood. Neil began to develop a deep desire to learn more about the "Jesus" some of the Christian kids talked about. He asked his rabbi some of his questions, but recalled, "he always intellectualized, never gave me good answers, and responded with great anathema toward my curiosity."

After leaving home for college, Neil grew distant from his Judaism, but after college married a Jewish girl and had an inspired career in the management side of radio and television media. The marriage did not last. He met his second wife, Anita, in Atlanta at a public relations party given by United Airlines. Anita was a Christian, but did not try to convert Neil. Yet he acknowledges "Anita's Christian belief and loving example were clearly the strongest factors in my coming to faith in Christ. Being next to her all those years, and seeing her complete trust in Christ—even when I was terminated three times in my business career—slowly drew me closer and closer to Jesus. I had never seen that kind of strength before."

Then in 1989 Neil was touched by the story of Dave Dravecky, just before experiencing the death of his mother, the loss of his job, and a total change of careers. During this time Anita asked Neil to come to church with her at a United Methodist church in Louisville. Shortly after, Wally Thomas, the pastor, offered to share breakfast with Neil on Wednesday mornings. They met weekly for over a year, and Neil unloaded all his stored-up questions from his childhood. He recalled, "I asked Wally hard questions and received direct answers back. And he was direct with me too, insisting that I begin reading and examining the Bible. He never once pushed the issue, and ... he always bought breakfast," Neil chuckled. "Then as I was reading the Sermon on the Mount in Matthew, something clicked in me. I fit Wesley's notion of prevenient grace to a T! No wonder I wound up becoming a Methodist," Neil exclaimed.

On November 30, 1991, Neil was baptized. Over the next three years he bore witness to many of his friends that Jesus was the Messiah, but none were more grateful than his older brother and his wife, who both came to a new encounter with God as they acknowledged and received Jesus as the Messiah and the Master Builder of their new lives of faith.

Neil's story bears witness to the truth that Kurt Kaiser names in his popular Christian song "Pass It On":

> That's how it is with God's love once you've experienced it;
> you spread his love to everyone; you want to pass it on.[17]

CHAPTER SIX

Becoming Better Carriers

"This is eternal life, that they may know you, the only true God, and
Jesus Christ whom you have sent."

—Jesus (John 17:3)

"Evangelism is one beggar telling another beggar where to find bread."

—D. T. Niles

Eternal life as defined and offered by Jesus to all humanity is
amazing grace. It is bread for the beggar, life and hope for the
dying, strength and meaning for every pilgrim, and a love song
tuned to every soul. Once we have experienced being touched by
this gift of God's love, we can't help but be changed. We may
stumble and fumble along the way, but we can never simply
return to the way things were. We have been "infected" with "faith,
hope and love, these three; and the greatest of these is love."[1]

Harry Poe in writing about the day of Pentecost has a wonderful
image of what the coming of the Holy Spirit did to change the lives
and focus of the early disciples.

Luke describes a sound like a rushing wind, accompanied by
tongues like fire that rested on everyone as a visible manifestation
of their possession by the Holy Spirit. In contrast to the torment
of those poor wretches described as "demon possessed," these fol-
lowers of Jesus were "God possessed."

No doubt the experience of Pentecost sealed the faith of the dis-
ciples in Jesus. With his resurrection, they still wondered whether
Jesus might now restore the ancient kingdom of Israel (Acts 1:6).
This view of the Messiah and his work saw salvation as a posses-

sion or commodity to which someone held title. With the coming of the Spirit, however, the disciples entered the new age they had not anticipated. Salvation meant incorporation into the kingdom of God, which occurred as the Holy Spirit swallowed them.[2]

This Spirit-saturated life form is the one designed and created by God and revealed in Jesus of Nazareth. Once we allow, by faith, this good infection to enter our hearts and heads and hands and feet, we are contagious. We are carriers. However, like those early disciples at Pentecost, there is still much our risen Lord has to teach us about how to "pass it on."

The purpose of this chapter is to bring together the theology and the survey data from previous chapters in lessons that will help us become better carriers. Unlike some other infections, the good infection is not able to be indiscriminately passed on. One does not usually "catch" it merely by being around someone who has it. A willing participation is required. The question then is this: How can we who long with all our hearts for others to be incorporated into this kingdom and find the bread of life, do all that is possible to enable them to choose to open their hearts to God and receive the divine gift of holy love?

A Personal Word About Carriers

One day as a nine-year-old walking home from Civic Park Elementary in Flint, Michigan, a friend asked me bluntly "Are you a Christian?" I responded, "Are you?" "Yes!" he declared with a note of absolute confidence. "Me too," I said, but with much less energy. Actually, my family was "unchurched" and I had no real idea what a Christian was except by my own definition, which went something like—"a good person who believed in God." My young companion, perhaps sensing my less than exuberant response to his inquiry, decided to shoot another query in my direction. "When were you baptized?" he asked, no doubt revealing something about his denomination's understanding of this sacrament. "When were you baptized?" I countered. "Yesterday!" he declared, once more with that same annoying confidence. And again, he asked me about my baptismal date. Not knowing how to answer, I honestly replied "I don't remember." "You don't remember?!" he countered

136

incredulously. With a bit of irritation beginning to show in my voice I confirmed again my lack of certainty. His next words turned the heat up even more. "I bet you're not baptized." "I am too," I shot back. "I bet you're not a Christian." "I am too!" I proudly—but ignorantly—declared.

Thus began my introduction to evangelism and Christian witnessing. Some might say my young friend was abrasive. Others might admire him for his bold witness. I initially only found him "a pain." But looking back with the benefit of hindsight, I know now he was a blessed point of contact in my life with God's grace. As I bolted into the house I greeted my mother immediately with an irritated mandate: "When was I baptized?" Over the course of the next few weeks my family began to attend church, and several months later, at the age of ten, I was baptized at Community Presbyterian Church. The infection had begun, and God's contagious carrier was a nine-year-old school chum.

Other "carriers" who enabled this small, initial infection to grow through its stages of faith include my mother who taught me early that God was interested in me and answered prayers; my sister who manifested a new spirit of love and spoke boldly of God being "real" after returning from church camp as a teenager; the leaders of that camp who challenged me the next year to seek God's presence and surrender myself wholly to Christ; pastors, Sunday school teachers, and youth counselors who prompted me to listen carefully to what God might be saying about my calling (though I surely didn't want to be a preacher); my college friend Eddie Waxer, who as a Jewish seeker after God discovered Jesus was his messiah and led me to see the difference between a merit-driven "commitment" orientation to Christian living, and an "indwelling Christ" orientation; and both of my parents and others who in tasting the reality of the Holy Spirit urged me to truly become acquainted with God the Holy Trinity. To this list a multitude of others could be added: friends, Christian writers, professors, colleagues, evangelists, missionaries, my wife and children. The good infection grows! Many play a part as carriers. The part is not always the same, but each part played is used by the Holy Spirit to lead us "from one degree of glory to another."

Evangelism Reexamined

This whole book has been an effort to explore what it is that God desires us to "catch," and how we can better serve as carriers of this wondrous offering of divine love that allows us to know God. Historically this effort of becoming better carriers of the gospel has been called evangelism or evangelization. Literally, evangelism is the verb form of the noun "gospel" (good news), and means "to gospel." Thus, we have translated the verb in English as to "declare" or "deliver" or "tell" or most commonly to "preach" the good news. These are adequate translations in some ways, but not very good descriptions of what we really are about as "carriers." To carry this gospel and pass it on contagiously is about more than "telling" and certainly about more than the activity we normally associate only with clergy—"preaching." If we can learn anything from scripture, tradition, reason, and experience it is that effective evangelism and Christian witness are mostly about being like Jesus.

This does not mean there aren't specific activities involved, nor that evangelism is only about being and not about doing or telling. As I write this, a WWJD bracelet lies before me. Strange how some things get recycled. The question "What Would Jesus Do?" first emerged as a challenge the Reverend Henry Maxwell gave to his "First Church" members in Charles Sheldon's classic novel, *In His Steps,* published one hundred years ago.[3] Today the WWJD has reemerged on the wrists of hundreds of thousands of young people because one youth group in Michigan decided to rekindle the challenge of living Sheldon's experiment of "earnestly and honestly for one entire year, not to do anything without first asking the question, 'What would Jesus do?' " Wearing the bracelet does not by itself make one a "carrier," but living as persons who desire to manifest the Spirit of Jesus in every activity does. To do what he would do and say what he would say is the essence of a truly contagious Christian witness, and evangelism is only as effective as the Christian witness out of which it grows.

For this reason most leaders in the field over the last thirty years have moved away from training Christian witnesses as "parrots" who memorize a standard presentation of the gospel or as "sales personnel" who are trained to close a deal. Being able to explain the gospel and invite others to respond to Christ's invitation to "come unto me" is important. Many devoted Christian lay persons and even pastors suffer from almost absolute ignorance of how to do either of these things in a face-to-face conversation with a person hungry for God.[4] More will be said later about helping to correct this problem. But because the gospel's goal is more about helping persons become eternally connected with God through receiving the life of Christ than it is about getting persons to believe a "plan of salvation" or go through a "rite of initiation," evangelism is by its very nature the ultimate relational act. Christians who effectively help others find life with God through an intimate acquaintance with Jesus Christ as Savior and Lord are Christians who first and foremost are rooted and grounded in the divine love. Then, following the guidance of the Holy Spirit, they share words and deeds that manifest this life of grace as they invite others to "come home" and "join the dance."

Contagious Christian witness is the larger arena in which the more specialized activity called evangelism takes place. Contagious Christian witness involves all we do to the glory of God as agents of grace, mercy, truth, justice, and love. Evangelism is more specifically related to communicating to others how they can join us in the Christian experience. One without the other, no matter which comes first, usually is inadequate to produce fully functioning Christian disciples who themselves desire to pass on the good infection. The remainder of this chapter offers guidance and suggestions for both activities.

So Then, What's a Parent to Do?

Let's begin where most Christians begin—in families of faith. Parents more than any other persons impact our perceptions of reality. This should not be surprising to anyone. In fact it would be a surprise if this were not the case, and, sadly, that surprise is already here. Considering today's changing shape of family life—the alarming percentages of children living without parental continuity, in single-parent settings, and in blended families—more and more of the traditional role of parents as "contagious good infection carriers number one" is going to have to be assumed by others. This is today's reality.

What's a parent to do? Several things can be gleaned from the life stories examined in this study.

First, Christian parents need to be reminded of how significant they are in the faith process of their children. Sometimes they won't believe it. Sometimes they would prefer not to believe it. Always they will need help and maybe even instruction regarding how to live out their lives as contagious carriers of faith. Perhaps more than ever before we need each other as Christian parents. Books like this one and a host of others need to be read and discussed in classes, seminars, circles, and home groups so that we can be informed, encouraged, and focused on our most important task as parents.

Second, Christian parents need to manifest love for God, love for their children, and love for others. This seems almost too obvious and far too easy to say, and we all know it is not always easy to do. Every sincere and honest parent can remember multiple times when this ideal slipped and both actions and words revealed a part of the parent's soul that was stressed, stretched, and maybe even sinful. These memories hurt. They hurt the child too. But, though we may fail—will fail—to always communicate God's grace-filled love, how we respond to that failure is part of the faith-modeling that matters. Acknowledge the failure, ask for forgiveness if necessary, pray together, look at a Bible passage that reminds us that when we fail God remains faithful to forgive us and restore us.[5] Parental faith-modeling is about the stuff of real living with all its ups and downs, but with an awareness that our relationship with Christ is always the highest priority and the larger reality we are called to manifest.

Third, Christian parents need to recognize that they have the primary responsibility for instructing their children in matters of faith.

> You shall love the LORD your God with all your heart, and with all your soul, and with all your might. Keep these words that I am commanding you today in your heart. Recite them to your children and talk about them when you are at home and when you are away, when you lie down and when you rise. (Deuteronomy 6:5-7)

In America and elsewhere many parents of the post-World War II Boomer generation abandoned this task. As they left behind their own early religious training searching for alternative forms of meaning, they had little to offer their children except a vague "make your own choices" mantra. Even as many of these parents returned to church, they were essentially looking for their own answers and not ready to take the lead for their children. Besides, many of their children were already "carefully taught" not to expect much from God, the church, or the Bible, even if they still held some form of theistic belief. Thus, many of today's young parents, children of the Boomers, have been robbed of their inheritance and have little to pass on to their young children. This is why it is critical that they obtain assistance to retake their rightful and biblical place in God's design for parents.[6]

This may especially need to be emphasized for today's fathers. Research has shown at least two important trends: (1) a father's attendance at church is a key predictor of the future church participation of his children[7], and (2) fathers are only half as likely as mothers to be listed as persons of "contagious influence" by participants in the Asbury Study. This is not the place to examine "why" fathers have seemingly neglected their proper place as spiritual role models,[8] but it is an appropriate place to put in a plug for every effort that is enabling young men and old, husbands and fathers, to once again claim their God-given spiritual identity for both themselves and for their families.

Fourth, although it is important that Christian parents model their faith and guide their children in understanding and responding to the gospel, it does take a village—a Christian community, maybe especially today—to raise a child. This is true for younger children, but it is especially true for children as they pass through adolescence. Others who teach the Bible, others who model their faith, others who speak of their Christian experience and daily walk with Christ, others who pray with us and for us are clearly part of God's carriers of faith. Parents are most critical in the early years. As children begin school and associate more and more with peers, programs at church become more and more important to provide the guidance, support, and discovery opportunities they will need to live as committed Christians in a society that increasingly devalues much of what Christ intends for those who claim to be his. Support from this kind of peer group becomes especially important during adolescence. Research shows that these are the church attendance "drop out" years, especially in families where "Dad" is not active. A distinct advantage for remaining active as adults belongs to those who were involved in church "two to three times a month or more" as seniors in high school.[9]

Fifth, and what may appear to be "stretching it," this father has discovered how important it is to speak of our Christian life and faith in relation to all three persons of the Trinity. To speak only of "God" or "our heavenly Father," or only of "Jesus" or "Christ," or only of the "Spirit" neglects the fullness of our faith and reduces the divine dance of God into a one-step or two-step. Each of us as individuals and as members of our respective traditions has a favorite or natural vocabulary related to God. But we do an injustice to God's self-revelation and to scripture if we neglect to let our language reflect all of the divine life offered to us by the mystery of God as Holy Trinity. Try it. What is the natural "God language" you use? Why? What would happen if you stretched your witness to look more like that found in the testimony of the early church? Read again a few chapters in the book of Acts or one of Paul's letters. Our children deserve a chance to become familiar with the full vocabulary and the all embracing reality of the wonderful dynamic of divine love revealed as "Father, Son, and Holy Spirit."

Sixth, Christian parents need to make sure they are allowing their children to experience the importance of being needed, not just having their needs met. As parents we will certainly want to tell and show our children we love them, but we also need to help them learn the joy of giving, not just receiving. This "ministry and mission" focus is often neglected. We too often believe our task as parents and the task of our Sunday school classes is to train children in what to believe and how to behave. As important as this task is, Jesus told his disciples to "make disciples" by "teaching them to obey everything I have command you" (Matthew 28:20). He said this was the source of his joy, and would be the source of our joy too as we lived in intimate union with him and loved one another (John 15:1-11). All of us, children and youth included, need to know that our lives can make a meaningful difference in the lives of others. For children, this can include but should never be restricted to a valentine for Mom and an Easter card for Grampa. Learning to give to others in ministry and mission out of the overflow we have received is the essence of Christian stewardship, and critical to the discovery that each one of us is important to the kingdom of God.

What's a Friend to Do?

No matter our age, having a real friend is important. We all are touched by the television commercials showing little girls or boys as the best of friends who years later "reach out and touch." Friends also help us "reach up and touch." For those making significant faith decisions in childhood, friends only account for one or two percent of the "most influential" agents. But as noted in Chapters 4 and 5, faith-contagious friends are far more important carriers for teenagers and adults. By late adolescence and through the thirty-somethings, friends are the dominant persons influencing our interest in finding a life connected to God. The level of this influence seems to peak during the "on my own" years between ages eighteen and twenty-five. So, what are we to do as friends of Jesus and friends of those who do not yet know him as their ultimate best friend?

First, be a true friend. As simple as that sounds, true friendship is not simple or easy. The model is Jesus himself. "As the Father has loved me, so I have loved you.... No one has greater love than this, to lay down one's life for one's friends. You are my friends" (John 15:9, 13, 14). Joseph Scriven captures it well.

> What a friend we have in Jesus, all our sins and griefs to bear!...
> Have we trials and temptations? Is there trouble anywhere?
> We should never be discouraged; take it to the Lord in prayer.
> Can we find a friend so faithful who will all our sorrows share?
> Jesus knows our every weakness; take it to the Lord in prayer.[10]

A friend does not depart in times of sorrow, trouble, or trial, but rather lends a hand, a shoulder, an ear, a heart. When we maintain our friendship with Jesus as primary, we are able and ready to be a true friend to others.

Not every religious or secular definition of friendship is appropriate for Christian witnessing. Some offer counsel sounding much like this from the Koran. "Take not the Jews and the Christian for friends.... Choose not your fathers nor your brothers for friends if they take pleasure in disbelief rather than faith."[11] Often we choose friends because they are like us or based on what we think they can do for us. Christian carriers will have a variety of friends including several who do not share their perspectives or experiences of faith. These are persons for whom Christ came to earth, died, and rose again, and persons whom the Holy Spirit is drawing toward God. True friendship has the welfare of the other at heart, and nothing a friend can do is of greater significance than being an instrument of God's grace.

Second, be ready to engage in spiritual conversations and invite your friend to join you in an experience of Christian community. To share in spiritual conversations does not mean to perform an inquisition about your friend's beliefs or to attack his or her values or ethics (or lack of them). However, neither does it mean being passive, never taking the initiative because you are afraid of being thought "pushy." It means being natural and honest. That's how friends are with each other. The events and issues that naturally shape our thoughts and conversations always lead sooner or later to opportunities for sharing matters of faith and especially the priority of our relationship with Christ. These are often times for asking "What is your own highest priority?" "How do you make tough decisions?" or "When have you felt closest to God?" Accept the answers, whatever they might be, as a friend. But don't be afraid to invite your friend to church or to a small group of some kind where others will honestly seek answers and open themselves to God's presence and to the Bible. According to research by George Gallup, Jr., 62% of "unchurched" Americans say no one has asked them to attend church during the past year. Half of these can readily picture themselves enjoying their participation if invited by the right person. Be that person. Invite a friend to take a step, any step, closer to Christ and the fellowship of his body.

Third, offer Christ. We are not carriers of "church" or "religion" in general, but carriers of the Christ life available to all who will surrender their own self-imposed poverty for the riches of amazing grace and the gift of the Holy Spirit. Take advantage of opportunities your church offers to learn more about how to clarify the good news of God's love and redeeming grace. Learn how to invite them not only to join you at church, but how to open their lives to Christ. Sometimes, we can't answer all their questions or address all of their concerns, but we can take them seriously. Perhaps they would like to have a conversation with a pastor or other church leader. Perhaps a book or a cassette tape or a video would be helpful. Maybe they would like to join you at a Bible study or Sunday school class. Ask, but don't push. Be patient, but persistent. Introduce your friend to Christ the friend of all.

Fourth, help your friend meet and relate to other Christians. Very few of us make lasting decisions about our faith in isolation, nor should we. This is especially true of biblical faith, which reminds us that we are meant to be the people of God, the body of Christ, the church of God. Too many "believers" in America today have been wrongly led to believe that they can be "Christians" and yet have no corporate dimension to their faith. In the first place those who are still evaluating the meaning of the gospel for their lives need to witness the power of Christian unity in diversity. They need to know that they can still be themselves, unique as human beings, even after they surrender their wills to the will of God and become one with Christ. It doesn't really matter whether the setting is a discussion group, a softball team, or a Habitat for Humanity task force. The more varieties of the common contagious strain called "Christian" they experience, the more they will recognize there is freedom in being bound to the love of God. Secondly, since the desired outcome is their full participation in the kingdom of God in the body of Christ, they need to get acquainted with their brothers and sisters in the family.

Fifth, pray. There is a profound mystery involved in prayer. During a recent "Youth Sunday" worship experience a young woman began to lead us in the Lord's Prayer—"Our Father, who art in heaven..." Suddenly, a voice came over the PA. "Yes, you called?" All of us were taken by surprise. For the next several minutes we listened in on a conversation between the young woman and "God" as she (and we) had our eyes opened to what it truly meant to pray the Lord's Prayer rather than just say it. At times our prayers are merely perfunctory, at other times they sound as if we are trying to change God's mind. But when we pray for the conversion of a friend, we are in perfect harmony with God's will, who desires no one "to perish, but all to come to repentance" (2 Peter 3:9). Our prayers are united with those of Jesus himself—what a mystery— who prayed (John 17:20) and prays (Romans 8:34) for us and for them.

There is much we will never know about the power of prayer as it relates to Christian witness. But the curtains of heaven were pulled back for me to catch a glimpse of this mystery when I shared the song, "That's Me Without God," written by David Withers (Chapter 4), with a small church in Seltzer Springs, Kansas. It had been several months since my encounter with David and his joyful reunion with Christ. Immediately following the service, a woman rushed to greet me and excitedly announced "I know David Withers! I know his mother and his father and his whole family. We've been praying for David for six years!" I was humbled. I had been only one of God's many instruments in David's life. And in fact, my part was the smaller part; the faithful prayers of those who loved him, though they had lost track of him, were the greater part. As friends, let us pray "without ceasing."[12]

What's a Church Leader to Do?

Pastors and other Christian workers have the responsibility of helping those entrusted to their care to:

> no longer be children, tossed to and fro and blown about by every wind of doctrine.... But speaking the truth in love, we must grow up in every way into him who is the head, into Christ, from whom the whole body, joined and knit together by every ligament with which it is equipped, as each part is working properly, promotes the body's growth in building itself up in love. (Ephesians 4:14-16)

How should a pastor, in light of the insights that have emerged from the Asbury Study, lead a congregation to build itself up in love? How should a pastor and other congregational leaders model the contagious Christian life and provide for effective ministries of Christian witness and evangelism that will help spread the good infection of the new creation?

First, church leaders are responsible to reveal their own contagious life of Christian love. Whatever gifts one might have or bring to leadership in the church, "if I ... have not love, I am a noisy gong or a clanging cymbal" (1 Corinthians 13:1). Pastors, Sunday school teachers, youth leaders, and even visiting evangelists are recognized as most influential in helping others catch the faith if they manifest a winsome, honest, obvious, personal relationship with Christ. We need to be encouraged to talk openly and honestly about our own life with God. This does not "turn others off" but serves as a reminder that God is at work through grace for all of us, and none of us becomes a contagious person of divine love by being "born that way." The Christian life is a journey with significant and often unexpected discoveries, decisions, and life-changing moments along the way, and it continues every day we rise to face a new morning. Some of us need help here. We would rather "show" than we would "tell." But both are important ways of revealing how utterly dependent we are on God's amazing grace and not on our own personalities or power. There is much skepticism as well as spiritual hunger in our world today. Therefore, it is true that people won't care how much we know until they know how much we care.

Second, both pastors and lay leaders in our churches need to encourage, to hold accountable, and to pray for each other's contagious Christian witness in that Monday through Saturday world where we all live. If we only talk to each other on Sundays and Wednesdays about God's "amazing grace" it will cease to seem so amazing. Those who most want to make a difference in their churches will also model that "church" is not the only place God intends for us to care for others, communicate our love for God, or offer persons in spiritual darkness an opportunity to respond to the light.

I was speaking at a training event for pastors and lay persons in the mountains of eastern Oregon. One workshop on personal evangelism and witnessing was led by a middle-aged man who had just recently become a pastor. He offered to his workshop what he had learned as lay person who thought sharing his faith day in and day out was just what was expected of all Christians. Inspired and maybe even a little embarrassed by this lay-pastor's simple boldness, a sharp young minister confessed: "I'm an evangelist for flying single-engine planes, for cross-country skiing, and for mountain backpacking. I would like to be an evangelist for Jesus, and that's what my members think I learned in seminary. But they are wrong. If we're going to get the job done, and my people are waiting for me, we've all got a lot of work ahead of us. But I think it's about time we got started together."

That's the spirit more of us need. We don't need more blame, but we do need encouragement so we can help each other be more naturally involved in living and speaking to this contagious life every day. As we step out together in this endeavor, we will find it can actually be exhilarating and give us a fresh sense of learning to follow the leading of the Holy Spirit. In fact, if we don't step out together, can we ever really know what it means to belong to Christ?

Paul reminded his dear friend Philemon and those who worshiped with him in his house, "I pray that you may be active in sharing your faith, so that you will have a full understanding of every good thing we have in Christ." (Philemon 6, NIV) As Christians we can never really understand or experience what our faith in Christ is all about unless we share it. Spiritual growth and Christian witnessing are intimately connected. To separate them is to lose the life force each needs from the other. Perhaps this is close to the heart of the problem being experienced in many denominations today which seem to have lost their way.

Third, pastors, Sunday school teachers, and youth workers have special opportunities and responsibilities to explain to their constituents both the "what" and the "how" of this life-changing experience we call "coming to faith" or "Christian conversion." As gradual as arriving at mature faith may be, each of us needs repeated opportunities to respond to whatever it is that God is clarifying for us today. We who feel comfortable talking about the gospel, often are hesitant to invite those we address to take a step of faith into the fullness of a life in Christ. We assume that modeling and telling are enough. Not so. Although the Holy Spirit often works to confirm truth as God's word is expounded, evangelism involves the additional step of extending a non-manipulative invitation to receive the gift offered and not just hear about it or discuss it. Pastors and other Christian workers in every congregation should converse and pray with each other in order to clarify the approaches they will use for these invitations, and how they will follow up those who respond. Our ultimate goal can never be just a good sermon, lesson, or session. Rather, it must be to help lead others to truly encounter the living God of love, mercy, justice, forgiveness, and truth. "Ask, and you shall receive." (Matthew 7:7)

Fourth, congregational leaders in ministry need to be ready to make use of new programs that will give persons of all ages multiple opportunities to make discoveries and decisions about the gospel. Even as I write this paragraph I am 35,000 feet in the air over Kansas sitting next to an attractive, professionally dressed young woman on her way to the west coast. Diane, I discovered, is heading to Redwood City, California, for a computer program training presentation. After taking several years off to start her family (three daughters) she is back working part-time and juggling family commitments with her husband, who also travels. Diane is a lifelong

Roman Catholic who began during lunch to tell me about a program at her church called "First Place." "I think it's a Baptist program," she said, "but as Catholics we never really got much into Bible study. And this is a great program. It's about what you eat, how you treat your body, and your family, and your relationship with God." She told me they meet weekly to talk about eating right and living right; and each week they have Bible study and verses to memorize. "It's wonderful!" she exclaimed, and then confessed that even though she was feeling pressure about this trip, she took time this morning for her Bible study and prayer, and it helped!

We continued to talk about how various "programs" move across denominational boundaries these days. We talked about "Cursillo," "Walk to Emmaus" and "Marriage Encounter." Diane excitedly told me the most profound experience she and her husband had ever had was their Marriage Encounter weekend. They now meet faithfully once a month with a group of Christian couples who get together to refresh that common experience of Christ in their lives and their marriages. She admitted, "I'm always trying now to help others find this in their lives, and the easiest way I know is for them to attend a weekend too. I'm a recruiter!"

Diane was a "contagious carrier." I was blessed by her witness and reminded that God's design for our lives is full of such serendipity, even at 35,000 feet. But how did Diane's life jump from a faithful "attendee" to a "contagious carrier"? She was given a chance to participate in a church program related to something the Holy Spirit had been nudging her to consider for a long time. Many, in fact most, persons make their initial discoveries of transforming faith while participating in their own churches. Some would say this seems backwards. First get them converted, then they can join the church. However, "conversion" for most of us is a collection of experiences, not a single event. It is "from one degree of glory to another" (2 Corinthians 3:17) that we "are being saved" (1 Corinthians 1:18). Each time I gave myself to Christ it was with as much as I knew how to give at the moment. Each time I received God's gift of saving grace, it was with as much as I was ready for at the moment. A danger for us all is to think "it is finished" after one of these sacred moments. In reality, many of us need several steps to truly get across the line into a life of contagious Christian living. Church leaders need to regularly offer new programs and invitations so that persons can take another step of faith as they are ready. Children, youth, adolescent girls, adolescent boys, young adults, new-lyweds, parents, older adults—whatever the age or stage, we need to design new occasions for God's children to say "yes" to the gift of eternal life. Such invitations should be sincerely offered Sunday after Sunday as well as during occasional special programs. Churched and unchurched alike need to be "invited," for Catholics and Methodists, Presbyterians and Baptists, actives and inactives, orthodox and agnostics are all still in need of "experiencing God."[13]

Fifth, pastors, youth workers, and Sunday school teachers need to be reminded of the special role they play in assisting parents in the second stage of helping children and youth make faith decisions. Any parent who has been praying and working for a child to decide for Christ and experience God's saving grace recognizes how very important other adults in the church are to this process. Pastors and youth workers are especially important. The older the children in our churches are before this reality becomes their own, the more important the role an adult "counselor" becomes. Confirmation classes and baptismal instruction are important. But unhurried, non-manipulative, focused moments of face-to-face, heart-to-heart listening, sharing, and praying with these young brothers and sisters is critical in passing on the gift. Are there a variety of adult workers who are trained and ready to assume this role? Although some youth will make these significant decisions alone and sense that only God was there in the moment of faith and surrender, most converts say the pastor or some other person was a critical agent used by God to enable this personal awareness of divine love and the assurance of eternal life. Are we talking about this in our churches? Are we helping those who work with all ages, and especially those who work with our children and youth, to know how to "explain the gospel"[14] and help another person claim in prayer the gift of divine love?

Sixth, a pastor or staff member and several key lay leaders should be involved in providing training for parents and the church workers described above. There are really two levels of training needed. One is focused on enabling every Christian to become a more contagious carrier, a better Christian witness. The model most helpful here is the one first set forth by the Apostle Peter.

1. "In your hearts set apart Christ as Lord."
2. "Always be prepared to give an answer to everyone who asks you to give a reason for the hope that you have."

3. "Do this with gentleness and respect." (cf. 1 Peter 3:15, NIV)

Some churches are emphasizing this simple three-part model of Christian witness (with role playing) as early in their discipling process as their membership classes. Others add it as one of the early small group emphases (key word, emphases) for those who are beginning their life in Christ or for those moving ahead in their Christian discipleship. New Christians and those who have recently experienced the renewal of God's love and grace in their lives are prime candidates.

The second level of training needed goes beyond generic Christian witness to personal evangelism and includes learning how to explain the basic gospel message, how to answer some common questions that people ask, and how to help those who are ready open the door of faith to their Abba, Father, to Christ their Savior, and to the Holy Spirit. More will be said later about a generic model of this kind of training, but a multitude of excellent resources are now available through denominational offices, various large churches, and a variety of other parachurch organizations.[15] Many of these are "kits" which include helpful video presentations, participant workbooks, and separate leader guides. This level of training is not necessarily for everyone. But churches that are growing and reaching new people for the kingdom are very intentional about recapturing both of these levels of equipping laity for Christian witness and evangelism. Pastors need to take the lead "with gentleness and respect."

What's a Congregation to Do?

Reaching out to others with the gospel has never merely been the work of a few isolated individuals who are "into" that sort of thing. This contagious life of divine love is a communal experience and is designed to be taught, caught, and enhanced by our corporate life together. Many local churches and perhaps whole denominations need to reexamine their statements of purpose, their programs, and their priorities to see if they are clearly committed to functioning as contagious communities of the good infection. Excellent studies have been undertaken and a multitude of books have been written over the last quarter century defining the qualities and priorities that enable congregations to effectively reach out to others. There is no excuse today for an unfruitful congregation to ignore these resources and continue to perpetuate the barren status quo. To do so would amount to unfaithfulness, not just unfruitfulness. So, what's a congregation to do?

First, churches should be adding studies such as this one and studies of how to be effective faith-sharing communities to their standard curriculum. Perhaps this kind of effort needs to begin with a special task force, but it will never become contagious throughout an entire congregation by being restricted to "committee work." Working with the pastor, a leadership team needs to design a strategy to encourage both special and ongoing efforts to read the best new materials and evaluate congregational efforts in light of the insights gleaned. Study what is happening in our more secularized postmodern culture today. Study how persons are coming to new faith. Study how they best grow into mature disciples. Study how congregations that are most effective in reaching out to new "seekers" do it. Discuss the changes this might necessitate. Ask where and how in the overall life of your church new persons are coming to faith. Which agents are involved? Is this adequate? Are you losing people who start the faith journey but fail to stay with it? Why? These research efforts, though not exhaustive, are more than likely adequate to discover some significant concerns and celebrations. Both are important. Combined, they serve as a congregational checkup to establish an accurate picture of the health of a congregation. The question is, "Are we contagious to the glory of God?"

Second, decide as a congregation to prioritize outreach, evangelism, faith-sharing, and faith nurturing among the many reasons that might be given for your existence. Then continually evaluate your faithfulness as disciples of Christ in terms of your efforts to help others find God and catch the good infection. Even when we think this is our ultimate aim as a church, we often discover that no one is really monitoring our efforts or asking how each activity or program contributes to this goal. Asking such questions makes a difference. Uniting behind this purpose changes the whole mind set and spirit of a congregation. It allows us to talk about the spiritual life of our children, youth, and adults whenever we gather, rather than restricting this to the role of a single committee or staff member. It also makes reporting the new decisions and discoveries of faith an expected activity rather than a kind of interruption to the "regular business of the church."

Third, our churches need to become more intentionally "houses of prayer." Passing on this contagious life is not primarily our work. There is mystery involved in the way God's Spirit works with each person. There is much we don't know regardless of how much we study. But we do know that God honors the efforts of people who pray. Heartfelt seasons of congregational prayer remind us all, long-term members and first-time visitors, whose house it is and who gets the glory. I am suggesting more than prayer as a per-functory "quickie" at the beginning of worship or choir practice or the board meeting. What would it mean if we would even pray five minutes instead of thirty seconds in these settings? What would happen if we actually sought God's presence and listened for guid-ance as well as offering our petitions? What would happen if our petitions included persons in our families and social networks we longed to see find new hope and life through trusting Christ? Prob-ably, it would seem very awkward at first. But prayer is the path-way into the presence and into the power of God. Whatever else we do, if we do not pray, we do not allow the Spirit to speak or to work. This is our number-one task as the body of Christ and the people of God.

Terry Teykl, a United Methodist pastor who is now working full time helping churches in many denominations discover the renew-ing power of prayer, writes in his book, *Pray the Price:*

> As pastors, we must take at least some of the responsibility for the prayerlessness of our people. Just as our seminaries do not offer courses on prayer, most of our churches do not either. And if we are not teaching our people to pray, how and where do we expect them to learn? Prayer does not come naturally for most—even the disciples pleaded, "Lord, teach us to pray" (Luke 11:1). . . . Men, women, youth, children—they all have a significant part to play in fulfilling the Great Commission, but we must send them out with the proper training. . . . To pray the price means to make prayer training an integral part of church life. We must model it in our services, preach on it from the pulpit, offer classes on it for all ages, plan special seminars or work-shops around it, and weave it into everything we do.[16]

Fourth, remind each other, as the New Testament church so often did, that loving one another and loving strangers in your midst are marks of Christian witness and very important in the process of how we assist others to come to life-changing encounters with God's grace in Christ. What is meant by "loving one another"? Most of us know inherently what this looks like and what it doesn't. Nevertheless, like prayer, we sometimes assume far too much when we counsel "love your neighbor." Research by Win and Charles Arn and Carroll Nyquist has revealed there are considerable differences in how churches and whole denominations are perceived by both members and visitors when it comes to how well they love. A "Love/Care Quotient" (LCQ) was developed from surveys involving 168 churches from 39 denominations. Over 8,600 persons participated. The results:

> One unmistakable conclusion of the love research in the 168 churches is the direct relationship that exists between a loving church and a growing church. Each local church surveyed was asked to give its membership growth percentage rate during the last five years. In comparing growth rates with the LCQ scores, it was found that growing churches showed a significantly higher love quotient than churches which had declined during the past five years—regardless of denomination. Churches that have learned to love, and to share that love are growing. Churches lacking in love are usually declining. Love, in Jesus' name, attracts people.[17]

Love is able to be measured, and is measured consciously or unconsciously by persons we are seeking to reach for Christ.

Fifth, intentionally seek to invite into your fellowship those who don't have the benefit of a Christian family heritage or a church home. This includes adults but needs to focus especially on children and youth. Loving instruction and well-planned opportunities for unchurched children and young people to encounter faith models among their peers and interest-taking adults is a critical ingredient for catching both the possibility and the reality of a saving and transforming encounter with Jesus. This needs to be more than the annual Vacation Bible School, but not less. Who is taking responsibility for this effort throughout the year? What kinds of opportunities are provided for children and youth to be involved in faith-clarifying activities and in sincere but nonmanipulative invitations to respond to God's love in Christ? How are mature and Christ-centered adults and youth helping in this endeavor? How are they being trained and encouraged for their work? Are they aware that different emphases might be called for when relating to early adolescent boys versus early adolescent girls? Are there special opportunities for young adults to enjoy each other's company as well as to explore together the tough questions they are encountering and the meaning of the Bible for their daily lives? Are we assuming responsibility not only for those in our "neighborhood" but also for those "across the tracks" and "across the seas"? Perhaps no congregation can do everything necessary to reach out to the lost and uninvited, but every church can do something more. Surely these "little ones" are close to the heart of Jesus.[18]

Sixth, make the adjustments necessary to help these new persons feel wanted and welcomed. Reduce the barriers to participation and enhance the gatherings for worship and fellowship with them in mind. Rules and regulations that become more important than an eternal soul need to be reevaluated. Traditions and tastes that only refresh the few who can remember them need to be part of the flavoring we offer, but not the whole feast. What can we do for the glory of God that is new and different? What will help children and youth of this generation find church as their "home" and Christ as their Savior, friend, and source of hope and power for living? Does the dress code need to be changed? Would it ever be okay to get excited and make "noise" in worship in response to a musical offering by the children? Could testimonies occasionally be offered by new people (children, youth, adults) who didn't know all the "right" terms and were just beginning to become aware of new possibilities? The list of questions could certainly go on and on, but the issue is are we a congregation more interested in helping others than we are in satisfying ourselves. This is Christian faithfulness that connects us with the presence of Jesus and enables others to find him in our midst.

P.R.E.P.A.R.E. for Contagious Evangelism

Many excellent training programs are now available to assist both the bold and the bashful in becoming more effective communicators of the divine invitation to "come unto me." Based on insights from scripture, the Asbury Study, and other research on Christian conversion, three components are involved in effective

155

Christian evangelism: (1) vital Christian witnessing, (2) clear communication of the gospel message and (3) ongoing opportunities for faith development and growth in Christian discipleship.

The following **P. R. E. P. A. R. E.** model presents these three components of evangelism in one formula. Training related to the first component, Christian witnessing, should be available and emphasized for all Christians, and is represented in the model by the letters **P. R. E.** One facet of the second stage in this phase of training (learning to listen) might be to use the interview format found in Appendix A. Over the years, students involved in the Asbury Study used a similar instrument for "listening" to the faith stories of others and found it to be a profound experience both for the interviewer and the interviewee.

Training for the second component, clarifying and inviting response to the gospel, should be offered to all church leaders and teachers and to others who want to take their Christian witness to the next level. The letters **P. A. R.** in the model constitute the ingredients in this second level of training. This is the phase of training most often addressed by denominational and parachurch training programs aimed at personal evangelism.

The third component is that of providing for growth in discipleship, represented by the final **E.** in the model. Some argue that this responsibility belongs not to "evangelism" but to "Christian education" or "discipleship formation." To some extent I would agree, which is why it is only a single element in the formula. However, evangelism that doesn't include appreciation for and orientation to this ongoing process of dynamic transformation is something less than Christian and unwittingly terminates the spread of the good infection.

The table below clarifies the meaning of each of the ingredients in the model and the holistic integrity that is needed if we are to **P. R. E. P. A. R. E.** members of the body of Christ to be contagious carriers of the good infection.

P.R.E.P.A.R.E. Evangelism Training

The Component		The Task	The Training
S T A G E **O N E**	O F F E R I N G O U R W I T N E S S	**P.** **Prioritize** your relationship with Christ.	Developing spiritual disciplines including regular participation in worship, devotional Bible reading, a small group, and prayer. These "habits of highly effective carriers" enable the witnesses to "abide in Christ" and reveal to others an authentic, living relationship with God the Holy Trinity.
		R. **Relate** as a true friend, in Christian love.	Learning to listen attentively and discern the life issues at work in people's lives. Readings, field assignments, and role-playing experiences enable witnesses to understand how both words and actions are important in communicating love for those God places in their path.
		E. **Explain** the reason for your hope.	Learning to share meaningful and relevant personal testimony at appropriate moments. Exercises, role playing, and field experiences enable witnesses to discover how to share expressions of their own story of faith in God.
S T A G E **T W O**	O F F E R I N G T H E G O S P E L	**P.** **Present** the gospel and offer Christ.	Learning to be sensitive to the Holy Spirit's leading and to clarify the gospel—offering Christ to persons seeking God. Bible study, exercises, role playing, and field experiences enable witnesses to discover how to share not only their story but the gospel story. Sometimes this is best done in groups.[19]
		A. **Ask** for a response.	Learning how to discuss the implications of the gospel and to invite persons to respond to God's offer in Christ. Bible study, exercises, role playing, and prayer assist the witness to discern the readiness of another to take an appropriate step of faith.
		R. **Repeat** as often as necessary.	Learning how to patiently help others make their own true response of faith. Often this requires the witness to maintain vigilance in prayer and lovingly await the next opportunity for faith modeling and faith sharing. "No" often means, "Not just yet."
STAGE THREE GROWING IN GRACE		**E.** **Enable** saving faith to become mature	Offering opportunities for all new Christians to grow into mature disciples through appropriate personal instruction and nurture, accountability, and discovering for themselves the joy of being a contagious witness.

Preparing persons today to be involved in effective Christian witness and evangelism requires pastors and lay leaders who work hard to understand the changing face of contemporary society and who know the importance of "high touch" relationships in a "high tech" world. George Barna, one of today's most widely read pollsters and a churchman committed to reaching contemporary pre-Christians with the gospel, writes:

> Our own explorations suggest that perhaps the most promising approach to evangelism these days is what I refer to as "Socratic evangelism." Socrates, the great Greek teacher, ... understood that if the insights he wished to impart were to have lasting impact and personal meaning, the student had to arrive at the conclusion on his own, thus having intellectually and emotionally worked through the obstacles to embracing the answer. In other words, the Socratic approach allows a person to own the answer, rather than to merely parrot it.
>
> Rather than telling people the answer, you start by asking them for their version of the answer to the meaning of life and the existence of God.... Accept them as human beings who—like we were at one point in life—are actively searching for truth.
>
> Such an approach to evangelism raises several challenges for today's evangelists. First, it means that relationships are important.... Second, it means that the forum for evangelism may vary from case to case ... but personal interaction on key matters pertaining to truth, faith, and personal lifestyle is crucial for the conversion experience these days.... Third, the Socratic approach means that evangelism will take time.... Fourth, effective evangelism requires that an evangelist not be threatened by individuals who have a different theological perspective or worldview.... Fifth, effective evangelism requires that evangelists understand their faith sufficiently so that they can hear the words and concepts offered by the nonbeliever, relate those perspectives to the Christian worldview, and be able to ask focused questions about the person's views which lead the non-Christian to take the next step toward arriving at God's truth.[20]

It is always a new day for the gospel. History moves on; things change; people change. What remains the same is the wonder of coming to know the reality of "love divine all loves excelling" by trusting in Christ as Savior and Lord and opening to the indwelling presence of God's Holy Spirit. Communicating this possibility is the task and privilege of Christian witnesses. Other than discovering the life-changing power of this encounter for oneself, there is no greater joy than to help another find it. It is indeed a divine dance choreographed to all the music of heaven and earth, and our task is to go everywhere humming the melody and occasionally breaking forth in song as we share the music and the words of *the good infection.*

A Final Note

Recently I laid the emaciated body of a dear friend to rest in a cold grave and celebrated the arrival in heaven of his singing and dancing soul. Smith Hundley was forty-nine, too young to die from cancer. More than five hundred persons attended his funeral and were deeply moved as we celebrated his life and witness among us. During the last six months or so of his life we met together quite regularly for conversation, prayer, singing, and just plain loving. Smith asked me to do the "personal" part of his funeral service because, he said, "You understand all that Christ has come to mean to me." I did.

Smith was a successful senior vice president of one of our nation's largest banks. He was a good churchman, a dedicated husband, a devoted father to his three girls, and busy making a living and enjoying life. His wife, Claire, attended a Walk to Emmaus weekend retreat in 1986 and came back "different." He wasn't sure he had time for or interest in "that sort of Christianity." It seemed a little too "feelings" oriented for him. But to make his wife and some friends happy, he attended an Emmaus weekend late in 1987. In a quiet way something profound happened to my friend that weekend. He met his risen Lord along that road to Emmaus, and like so many others, came home "different." It took him a year to tell me about the difference, even though Claire noticed it right away. One day as we sat together quietly in a chapel, Smith said "I need to tell you how much Emmaus has meant to me and my life." I asked him what had changed. He replied, "I'm more open with my family and at work. There is a freedom I feel deep in my soul. And, I am constantly aware of God's love and the presence of Christ. I'll never be the same."

This new "infection of divine love" was put to the test. Just five years later Smith was diagnosed with a cancerous tumor in his eye. It was necessary to remove the eye. Four years later the cancer returned and lodged in his liver. Through it all, Smith continued to show others how to "sing the Lord's song in a foreign land" (Psalm 137:4). Actually, he always had difficulty carrying a tune, yet the new song in his heart spilled over everywhere, and especially when he worked his garden and mowed the lawn. His simple goal in life was to "do justice, and love kindness, and to walk humbly with your God" (Micah 6:8).

For his funeral service he wanted people to hear two of his favorite scriptures.

> Who will separate us from the love of Christ? Will hardship, or distress, or persecution, or famine, or nakedness, or peril, or sword? No, in all these things we are more than conquerors through him who loved us. For I am convinced that neither death, nor life, nor angels, nor rulers, nor things present, nor things to come, nor powers, nor height, nor depth, nor anything else in all creation, will be able to separate us from the love of God in Christ Jesus our Lord. (Romans 8:35, 37-39)

> For this reason I bow my knees before the Father, from whom every family in heaven and on earth takes its name. I pray that, according to the riches of his glory, he may grant that you may be strengthened in your inner being with power through his Spirit, and that Christ may dwell in your hearts through faith, as you are being rooted and grounded in love. I pray that you may have the power to comprehend, with all the saints, what is the breadth and length and height and depth, and to know the love of Christ that surpasses knowledge, so that you may be filled with all the fullness of God. (Ephesians 3:14-19)

In addition, he wanted the songs in his heart to fill the sanctuary; and they did.

In His time, in His time,
He makes all things beautiful in His time.
Lord, please show me every day, as you're teaching me your way,
That you do just what you say, in your time.[21]

As the deer panteth for the water,
So my soul longeth after Thee.

You alone are my heart's desire, and I long to worship Thee.
  You alone are my strength, my shield;
To you alone may my spirit yield.
  You alone are my heart's desire, and I long to worship Thee.[22]

I lift up my hands to the Lord
  Singing "I love you, Lord, I love you. . . ."[23]

This is the life that is eternal. This is the good infection that spreads wherever God's children sing the music and dance the dance. This is the "final note" we all are made for, and we are off key until we are tuned to its glorious sound of praise. Yet, many all around us have never heard the song, seen the dance, or caught the infection. What else can be said?

Carry on.

Interview Format

Religious Background

1. As a child and/or a youth, how many times a month did you attend church? _____
With whom? _____ Where?
_____ What denomination or tradition?
_____

2. Was this mostly a positive or mostly a negative influence on your life? _____

3. To what extent did your parent(s) serve as role models of the Christian faith? _____

4. Which persons *most* stimulated your *interest* in becoming a Christian? _____,
_____,
_____.

5. What was it about these persons that most stimulated your *interest* in becoming a Christian?
_____
_____.

Claiming Your Own Faith

6. How old were you when you believe you became a Christian?
_____ (Please explain.)

7. Is there a particular event or occasion you think of as your conversion or critical turning point in your relationship with Christ ?
_____ Yes _____ No

8. *If* "Yes," how old were you at this time? _____ (may/may not be same age as #6)

9. Where were you when this happened? _____
_____

10. Who were you with when this happened?
_____

11. What particular person *most* helped you arrive at this decision or discovery? _____
_____

12. What was it about this person that most helped you make this decision? _____
_____
_____

The Experience Remembered

13. *If you can remember,* what were you looking for or seeking? In other words, why did you become a Christian?_____
_____

14. Was there any special way you sense God had been leading you to this decision? _____
_____

15. What do you remember as the most important/helpful part of the gospel message for you?_____
_____

16. What special insights or feelings did you experience at this time?_____
_____

17. How do you generally refer to this event in your life? What do you call it? How do you describe it?
_____

Your Life Since Becoming a Christian

18. Since becoming a Christian, have there been times when your faith has been severely tested or even abandoned? (Please explain.)

_____

19. Have you had additional special experiences that have enlarged or confirmed your faith?
(Please explain) _____

_____

20. As a Christian, what are your greatest longings or concerns today? (Please explain) _____

21. Is there anything else about your story of faith that you would like to share?

22. Are there any comments you would like to make about this interview?

NOTES

Preface

1. Stephen R. Covey, *Spiritual Roots of Human Relations* (Salt Lake City, Utah: Deseret Book Company, 1970) p. 121.
2. The original interview model was developed in the early 1980s by Robin Wainwright, who was then teaching at Bethel Seminary in Saint Paul, Minnesota. In 1983 I began to make use of the model in evangelism classes taught at Asbury Theological Seminary. Through the years adjustments were made to the interview format, and computers were employed to process the growing body of data. Over two thousand Asbury students have contributed to this project by their interviewing efforts.
3. Colossians 1:27.

1. The Contagious God

1. The sense of utter smallness and insignificance experienced by the psalmist as he viewed the heavens changed to joy and praise as he realized that human beings were crowned with their own special glory and honor as children of God. Thus he celebrates with a grateful heart, singing "How majestic is thy name, O Lord, in all the earth" (verses 1 and 9).
2. "How Great Thou Art," words and music © Copyright 1953 S. K. Hine. Assigned to MANNA MUSIC, INC., 35255 Brooten Road, Pacific City, Ore. 97135. Renewed 1981. All rights reserved. Used by permission.
3. "In the Valley of the Shadow," *Parade Magazine* (March 10, 1996): 18-21.
4. 1 Corinthians 14:33.
5. See for example the resistance of Moses (Exodus 3 and 4); Jeremiah (Jeremiah 14-8; 20); Ezekiel (Ezekiel 2 and 3); and Jonah (Jonah 1). Perhaps Ezekiel's description is most poignant—"The spirit lifted me up and bore me away; I went in bitterness in the heat of my spirit, the hand of the Lord being strong upon me" (3:14).
6. As noted above in Luke 4 and in such passages as Matthew 5:17: "Do not think that I have come to abolish the law or the prophets: I have come not to abolish but to fulfill."
7. Rather than the traditional authority of a prophet, "Thus says the Lord," Jesus often uses expressions such as "But I say to you" and "I tell you." In Matthew's account of the Sermon of the Mount (chapters 5–7) these self-authoritative declarations occur no less than fourteen times. What's more, the whole section ends with the story Jesus tells about the wise man who builds his house upon the rock and adds, "And everyone who hears these words of *mine* [emphasis mine] and does not

act on them will be like a foolish man who built his house on sand" (7:26). No wonder "the crowds were astounded at his teaching, for he taught them as one having authority" (7:28-29). The issue of his "authority" (read by the religious leaders of his day as his arrogance and even blasphemy) becomes the line in the sand that alienates him from those who trusted in the prophetic tradition, but were not ready to hear God's voice in the first person singular spoken by a young man from Nazareth in Galilee.

8. These images come mostly from John's Gospel, but they are common. He is the Word of God who was in the beginning with God, and was God (John 1:1-2). Having seen his glory, we saw the Father's glory (1:14); and even more, though we have not seen God, he has made him known to us (1:18). And Jesus himself announces he has been sent from his Father in heaven (3:31-34) and to see him and know him is to see and know the Father (14:7-10).

9. The Psalms frequently call on God for judgment against evil and unrighteousness, and for justice on behalf of the meek and oppressed. God alone judges with complete righteousness and equity (Psalm 9:8), and "He shall judge between the nations" (Isaiah 2:4).

10. Note how often Paul trumpets this note (1 Thessalonians 3:13; 5:23; 2 Thessalonians 1:7-10; 1 Corinthians 1:8; 4:4-5; 5:5; 2 Corinthians 1:14; 5:10; Philippians 3:20; 4:5), and it is not lost to John's writings either (John 8:15; 9:39; 12:47-48).

11. Common in Acts (2:21; 4:12; 5:31; 14:23; 15:11), in Paul (Philippians 3:20; Ephesians 5:23), in the Johannine writings (John 4:42; 1 John 4:14; Revelation 7:10), and elsewhere (Hebrews 2:10; 5:9; 7:25; 9:28; 2 Peter 1:1; 2:20; 3:2, 18, etc.).

12. Considerable theological work has already been done on ascribing this designation to Jesus. The term (*kyrios,* meaning "Lord") is used 8,400 times in the Greek version of the Old Testament known as the Septuagint. Only about 400 of these are references to human beings. The remaining 8,000 are used to refer to God as the "LORD" (6,700 of 8,000 occurrences make it a substitute for the tetragram YHWH). In the context of Judaism, to say "Jesus is Lord" is paramount to saying Jesus is Yahweh. Nor is this announcement only a Greek addition. The popular language of Jewish Palestine was Aramaic, and Paul's expression "Maranatha" (1 Corinthians 16:22) is Aramaic for "Our Lord, come!"

13. By the second century there were many extracanonical writings that referred to Jesus as God (Didache 10:6; Pliny Ep.X. 96:7; Ignatius Eph. 1:1; 15:3; 18:2; and 19:3 just to name a few).

14. The quote about being "gods" originally comes from Psalm 82:6 and is used by Jesus in John 10:30-39 in his conversation with some of the Jews who wished to stone him because he committed blasphemy by claiming to be "one" with the Father. It would be important to examine how Jesus used this text before making too much of it as a claim that we are all "gods."

15. Charles W. Lowry, *The Trinity and Christian Devotion* (New York: Harper and Brothers, 1946), p. 22.

16. Thomas C. Oden, professor of theology at Drew University and renowned patristics scholar, has contributed an excellent resource for this discussion in volume one of his three-part systematic theology. He writes, "The earliest Christians were steeped in monotheistic faith, but they had to make sense out of the inescapable revelatory event—this living, resurrected presence of the Lord in their midst. They understood Jesus to be not a demi-god, not part God, not proximately similar to God, but in the fullest sense 'true God'.... This is the reason we have triune thinking. If the disciples had not had that fundamental experience, we would not be talking about the Trinity today." *The Living God* (San Francisco, Harper & Row, 1987), p. 184.

17. See St. Augustine "On the Trinity," especially Books VIII and IX in *The Nicene and Post-Nicene Fathers,* First Series, vol. 3, ed. Philip Schaff; available both in book form and in CD-ROM through Sage Digital Library Collections, SAGE Software, Albany, Ore., 1996.

18. Jonathan Edwards, *An Unpublished Essay of Edwards on the Trinity* (New York: Charles Scribner's Sons, 1903) with remarks by George P. Fisher.

19. Edwards, pp. 93-94.

20. Edwards, p. 79.

21. C. S. Lewis, *Mere Christianity* (New York: MacMillan Paperbacks Edition, 1960), pp. 151-52.

22. Lewis, p. 153.

23. One might even say that the primary role of the Old Testament prophets seems frequently to be that of marriage counselors engaged in reality therapy reminding God's people of their need to repent and reunite themselves in love and faithfulness to the one who loves them with an unending love. Read Jeremiah 2 and 3 along with Ezekiel 16 and all of Hosea to catch this recurring theme.

24. Lewis, *Mere Christianity,* p. 152.

25. "Lord of the Dance," words by Sydney Carter. Copyright © 1963 by Stainer and Bell Ltd. All rights reserved. Used by permission of Hope Publishing Co., Carol Stream, Ill. 60188.

2. The Good Infection

1. The Hebrew word for "presence" is *panim,* the plural form of "face." Thus, the presence of God is read literally as the "faces" of God. Here again we see the theme of unity in diversity. We all manifest one personality with multiple faces. The person is in the face(s) although the face is not the person. Our full presence is the sum of the faces, and more.

2. "Shalom"—well-being, blessedness, wholeness, restoration to the design of God for all creation.

3. "Meekness" is often confused with being withdrawn, mild-mannered, and soft or even spineless. My wife once remarked concerning Jesus' beatitude about the "meek inheriting the earth" (Matthew 5:5)—"It serves them right for keeping their mouths shut." The biblical concept of meekness is humility before God and willingness to be an obedient servant. It is the opposite of arrogance, not in weakness of will, but in purity of heart to make one's own will identical to the will of God. Similar qualities are expressed by being humble and "lowly" in bearing and simple in matters of creature comforts and self promotion. In this sense John the Baptist is "meek," but who could ever accuse him of being quiet or weak willed?

4. 1 Samuel 8.

5. 1 Samuel 9–11.

6. 2 Samuel 11

7. 2 Samuel 12 and Psalm 51.

8. See Psalm 145:10-13.

9. It is regrettable that the NRSV chooses to translate "one like a son of man" in its most generic form, "one like a human being," in this verse. Jesus selects this as his most preferred title, possibly because it does provide a clear link to Daniel's vision of the arrival of the King of Kings.

10. Likewise, the literal translation of this expression is better rendered the "Ancient of Days" and clearly refers to God—as clarified in the NRSV textual footnote.

11. Mark's Gospel sounds the same opening note but with an added phrase of ful-

fillment: "Jesus came ... saying, 'The time is fulfilled, the kingdom of God has come near; repent, and believe in the good news' " (Mark 1:15). Incidentally, this was the favorite text of John Wesley when he preached in the open air and began the evangelical revival that spread "scriptural holiness" throughout England. Luke's Gospel keeps the same opening theme with only a slight variation: "I must proclaim the good news of the kingdom of God to the other cities also; for I was sent for this purpose" (Luke 4:43).

12. What Matthew prefers to call the "kingdom of heaven" (with few exceptions such as Matthew 6:33) is identical to what Mark, Luke, John, Paul, and other New Testament writers call the "kingdom of God" or even after Christ's death and resurrection the "kingdom of his beloved Son" (Colossians 1:13) or the "eternal kingdom of our Lord and Savior Jesus Christ" (2 Peter 1:11).

13. But it is clear that the twenty-nine occurrences of "kingdom" appearing outside of the Gospels, pales in comparison to the 119 occurrences in the Gospels. The theme remains, but other notes emerge as the chorus spreads from Jerusalem to Judea to Samaria to the ends of the earth.

14. E. Stanley Jones, *The Unshakable Kingdom and The Unchanging Person* (Nashville: Abingdon Press, 1972), p. 75.

15. A reminder that the consequence of a broken covenant is death figures in God's judgment against King Zedekiah and all the holders of slaves who cut a covenant with the Lord to free their slaves; however, they free them only for appearances and then enslave them once more (Jeremiah 34:8-22). The word of the Lord to these faithless covenant breakers is "And those who transgressed my covenant and did not keep the terms of the covenant that they made before me, I will make like the calf when they cut it in two and passed between the parts" (Jeremiah 34:18).

16. Holiness is not merely a form of religious legalism and isolation from the temptations of the world; it is a life that manifests what it means to be "sanctified" or set apart as existing wholly for the glory of God. Holiness involves living in such close relationship to God that the purpose of God for all humanity is revealed as justice, mercy, goodness, truth, and love. Is such a thing possible for mere mortals? The good news of the new covenant says absolutely!

17. It is not possible to paint with these broad brushstrokes the intricacies of the new covenant related to the sacrifice of Jesus on the cross and the end of the old Jewish system of atonement through recognizing in repeated animal sacrifices that the "wages of sin is death" (Romans 6:23). Paul addresses this theme from time to time, but the entire letter to the Hebrews is designed to make clear for Jewish believers in Jesus as the Messiah that he is the fulfillment of the new covenant and the finalization of the old covenant.

18. This is the meaning of Paul's use of the term "flesh" as it appears in Romans 8. Apart from the gift of the Holy Spirit available to all who come to Christ in the new covenant, we are "only human"; and as history has proven, "flesh" tends either to disregard the law of God or to keep it only as a badge of self-righteousness.

19. True righteousness—rightness with God—comes not by effort, but by faith. See the criticism Jesus levels at those who believe that even the good practice of reading the Bible (rather than coming to him) is the way to eternal life (John 5:39-40). Both Jesus (Luke 4:25-30; 15:11-32; Matthew 20:1-16) and Paul (Romans 9:5 10:13) make it clear that being made right with God is a matter of God's mercy and our faith. Both Gentiles and others seen as "sinners" and "unworthy" will go in ahead of many who see themselves as the "faithful," if by that designation they also are not humbly trusting in God alone.

20. Literally, "according to the flesh."

21. E. Stanley Jones defined F.A.I.T.H. as "Forsaking-**A**ll-**I**-**T**ake-**H**im" (*Conversion,* Abingdon, 1959, p. 191). Faith is an intentional giving up of oneself, a letting go, an opening of the door of trust to future possibilities based on confidence in the one who asks for my heart and my hand. It is the stuff of a real marriage, and the stuff of real freedom and health in love and life. In some ways it remains as mysterious as the very promises it leads to—life, love, truth, hope, eternity. But it is the gate we have the key to open once we become aware of the truth of this gospel.

22. *Wesley's Works,* Journals, Vol. 1 (Grand Rapids: Baker Book House, 1978 reprinted from the 1872 edition issued by The Wesleyan Methodist Bookroom, London), p. 103.

23. *The Works of John Wesley,* Vol. 11: *The Appeals to Men of Reason and Religion and Certain Related Open Letters,* ed. Gerald R. Cragg (Nashville: Abingdon Press, 1992), p. 45.

24. Ibid., pp. 106-8.

25. Charles Wesley, *Hymns and Psalms, A Methodist and Ecumenical Hymn Book* (London: Methodist Publishing House, 1983), 793.

3. Catching the Faith as Children

1. This study conducted by the author and students in evangelism classes over the course of nearly fifteen years is the source of most of the data used to compose the remainder of this book, and is hereafter referred to as the "Asbury Study." A simplified version of the survey instrument can be found in Appendix A.

2. This name and all names used as illustrations in this and the following chapters are fictitious (unless used by permission) in order to protect the anonymity of those who shared their stories.

3. The expressions used by both groups to describe their childhood decision or experience were ranked as follows: (1) "saved"—34.4%, (2) "accepted Christ"—18.3%, (3) "became a Christian"—10.2%, and (4) "confirmed my faith"—4.9%. One interesting fact is that 13.4% of those who have *always* been Christians used the expression "confirmed my faith" while only 2.5% of those who identify *five to nine* as the years when they made their decision use this expression.

4. "Backsliding" or "sliding back" into old habits and patterns of sin, letting go of one's commitments and disciplines as a Christian is not a new term or a new experience. Many who described this experience actually used the term. Others may not have used the same expression, but clearly described similar experiences—usually as adolescents or young adults.

5. "Sacrament," from the Latin meaning "sacred moment."

6. Acts 2:38

7. A later study of 772 persons conducted in 1994 focused more specifically on this issue and discovered 48% who said they "had experienced another time later in life when they thought of themselves as having *really* become a Christian." Some who answered "yes" did not prefer the wording "*really* become a Christian," but did have an experience later in life when they decided to live intentionally as a Christian. The mean age for this second decision was 22.3 years with a range of ten to sixty-three. Early young adulthood appears to be a time of significant reevaluation of important decisions made earlier in life. It would be a shame to lose contact with our "churched children" during this stage of life.

8. The Salvation Army does not normally perform rites of baptism nor do they serve the sacrament of the Lord's Supper.

9. Although American citizens from over forty states ranging from Oregon to

Florida, and from Texas to Maine are represented in the study, and although internationals from more than thirty countries are included, the largest representations are from Kentucky (25%), Ohio (9%), Michigan (8%), and Indiana (7%). Other states with more than 2% include: Georgia, Illinois, North Carolina, Florida, Texas, Tennessee, New York, and Virginia.

10. Those who currently claim to be United Methodist represent 45% of the sample followed by "Other" (14.7%), Baptist (8.9%), Free Methodist (7.4%), Wesleyan (5.0%), Pentecostal (4.3%), Unaffiliated (4.1%), Christian & Missionary Alliance (2.6%), Presbyterian (2.1%), and with 2.0% or less Nazarene, Roman Catholic, Salvation Army, Lutheran, and Friends.

11. "Child of Blessing, Child of Promise," words by Ronald S. Cole-Turner, *The United Methodist Hymnal,* 611. Used by permission.

4. The Susceptible Years—Adolescence

1. Jacques Barzun, from the Foreword to the Mentor Edition, *The Varieties of Religious Experience* (New York: The New American Library of World Literature, 1958), p. vi.

2. Ibid., p. 141.

3. Ibid., p. 143.

4. James writes, "To be converted, to be regenerated, to receive grace, to experience religion, to gain an assurance, are so many phrases which denote the process, gradual or sudden, by which a self hitherto divided, and consciously wrong inferior and unhappy, becomes unified and consciously right superior and happy, in consequence of its firmer hold upon religious realities" (p. 157).

5. *The Psychology of Religion,* (New York: Charles Scribner's Sons, 1906).

6. See V. Bailey Gillespie's *Religious Conversion and Personal Identity* (Birmingham: Religious Education Press, 1979), p. 78. A study of 4,054 subjects by Hall in 1904 averaged 16.6 years, Athearn's study of 6,194 subjects in 1924 averaged 14.6 years, T.T. Clark's study in 1929 averaged 12.7 years, and Argyle found in 1959 the average to be about fifteen years.

7. "Adolescence" is defined in this study as the age range from ten to nineteen. Although some might prefer to set the onset of adolescence later or terminate the range at eighteen, or argue this range is too extensive, others would seek to extend it well into the twenties.

8. 1999 data estimates from the U.S. Census Bureau.

9. With the ease of access to the Internet, such reports and all the latest up-to-date data are at our fingertips. One helpful location for these youth studies is found on the World Wide Web at http://www.youthwork.com.

10. *Junior High Ministry* (Grand Rapids: Zondervan Youth Specialties, 1987), pp. 50-51.

11. Ibid., p. 128.

12. Quoted by Mike Yaconelli and Jim Burns in *High School Ministry* (Grand Rapids: Zondervan Youth Specialties, 1986), pp. 10-12.

13. *The Religious Life of Young Americans* (Princeton: The George Gallup International Institute, 1992), p. 23.

14. Recently a clergy friend of mine who was teaching a basic freshman course on the New Testament at a small church-related college recounted an experience from the opening day of class. He asked the thirty students assembled to record on a sheet of paper the name of all the books of the New Testament they could remember. The highest number identified by any of the "churched" students was nine.

Gallup reports in the *Young Americans* study that only 35% can name the four Gospels, 66% knew how many disciples Jesus had, and just 71% knew why Easter Sunday was important.

15. *Young Americans*, p. 27.

16. Ibid., p. 11.

17. *Monitoring the Future*, University of Michigan, Institute for Social Research, cited in *Youth Indicators 1996: Trends in the Well-Being of American Youth*, September 1996, http://www.ed.gov/NCES/pubs/yi

18. Gallup, *The Religious Life of Young Americans*, p. 13.

19. Average church attendance was described as at least one or two times a month, and significant attendance was three or more times a month. Average parental faith modeling consisted of occasional but not regular prayer times and/or grace at meals, Bible reading, conversations about Christian values, and making decisions accordingly. Significant parental faith modeling involved a consistent emphasis on these and other such habits, values, and disciplines.

20. *The Heart of Youth Ministry* (Wilmore, Ky.: Bristol Books, 1989), p. 47. These authors describe and have implemented an extremely effective evangelistic youth ministry built on the recognition that parents, pastors, youth workers, and peers all have a critical part to play in helping the Christian contagion become real for young people. My son Matthew is presently in full-time youth ministry largely because of the influence of this program and its authors.

21. Fathers are listed by only 3.2% of the subjects as their most important Christian models and by only 1.3% as the person leading them to a faith decision. Corresponding figures for mothers are 6.9% and 2.8%, or about twice as important.

22. "Teenagers Are Begging: 'Feel My Pain,' " *Decision* (Vol. 38, No. 1, January 1997), pp. 9-10.

23. A term used by one of the more than 500 subjects in a study undertaken by the British Bible Society, composed in a report written by John Finney, published in 1992 under the title *Finding Faith Today, How Does It Happen?*

24. James Fowler, *Stages of Faith* (San Francisco: Harper and Row, 1981).

25. *The Experience of Faith* (Birmingham: Religious Education Press, 1988) pp. 130-34. Reprinted by permission.

26. *alive now* (September/October 1979), p. 14.

27. According to James, conversion is the process "gradual or sudden, by which a self hitherto divided, and consciously wrong inferior and unhappy, becomes unified and consciously right superior and happy, in consequence of its firmer hold upon religious realities." *Varieties*, p. 157.

28. *The Experience of Faith*, p. 114.

29. *The Experience of Faith*, pp. 162-63.

30. Omer Westendorf, "Where Charity and Love Prevail." Translated from ninth-century Latin. Copyright 1961 by Word Library Publications, Inc. *The United Methodist Hymnal* (Nashville, 1989), 549.

5. Coming to Faith as Adults

1. Jürgen Moltmann, *The Church in the Power of the Spirit* (New York, Harper & Row, 1977), p. iii.

2. Kerr and Mulder, *Conversions* (Grand Rapids: Eerdmans, 1983). Beginning with the Apostle Paul and tracing history through Constantine, Augustine, Teresa of Avila, Blaise Pascal, John Wesley, Sojourner Truth, Leo Tolstoy, E. Stanley Jones, Ethel Waters, Eldridge Cleaver, and Charles Colson—to name just a few—

reminds the reader that the God of the Bible is ever working through the Holy Spirit to bring mature men and women to a transforming encounter with Jesus Christ.

3. Charles Colson, *Born Again* (Old Tappan, N.J., Chosen Books, 1976), pp. 109-17.

4. *Surprised by Joy* (London: Fontana Books, Collins Press, 1955), pp. 182-89.

5. *The Guideposts Treasury of Love,* (Carmel, N.Y., *Guideposts,* 1978), pp. 123-26.

6. For example, Gary McIntosh in his book *Three Generations: Riding the Wave of Change in Your Church* (Grand Rapids, Revell, 1995) also calls the "Builder" generation "Strivers" and "Survivors." The "Builder" generation as a whole is described normally as those born prior to 1945 (although some say the cut off is 1943). McIntosh further divides "Builders" into "The GI Generation" (born prior to 1925), "The Silent Generation" (born between 1925 and 1939), and "The War Babies" (born 1940 to 1945). "Boomers" are likewise divided into "The Leading-Edge Boomers" (1946–1955) and "The Trailing-Edge Boomers" (1956–1964). The variations are relatively minor, but still myriad. All in all, however, the idea of three generations pre-WWII, post-WWII, and 1965–83 basically defines today's adult population.

7. (New York: William Morrow, 1991), p. 429.

8. Finney, *Finding Faith Today,* p. 42.

9. The results of this fascinating study conducted among 92 Estonian and 142 Russian-speaking persons who became Christians in Estonia after the collapse of the Soviet Union are presented in Griffin's D.Min. dissertation "Christian Conversion in Postcommunist Estonia," Asbury Theological Seminary, 1995.

10. Finney, *Finding Faith Today,* p. 43.

11. Woody Davis studied what brought men to faith and active participation in church. He writes "Far and away the most frequently mentioned variables were relational. Time and again the words love, concern, acceptance, and unity came up." ("Men and the Church," in *The Journal of the Academy for Evangelism in Theological Education,* 3, (1987–1988): 54).

12. This statistic could be somewhat misleading, however, at least with regard to the "general Christian population." Since nearly a quarter of all those interviewed were Christian college or seminary students, pastors, or professors, it becomes important to look at the remaining 75% of the sample. Here only about 20% report having experienced a "special call" from God for their work or ministry. But even this corrected figure means that at least one in five Christian converts report sensing God's direction for their life's work or for special ministries.

13. *Varieties,* p. 216.

14. Ibid., pp. 219-20.

15. A "saint" is one "sanctified" or "holy" or "wholly set apart for the glory of God." The New Testament calls all Christians "saints" not merely a few who seem to be specially graced.

16. Leslie Church in *The Early Methodist People,* reports that the large Foundry Society in London, reported 2,200 members but had only 639 in the bands (small groups focused specifically on Christian maturity). To be in a band required, among other things, that "you have the witness of God's Spirit," "the love of God shed abroad in your heart," and that "no sin, inward or outward, has dominion over you." Of the 639 in the Bands, 300 were on "probation."

17. Kurt Kaiser, "Pass It On," Copyright 1969 by Communiqué Music. *The United Methodist Hymnal* (Nashville, 1989), 572.

6. Becoming Better Carriers

1. 1 Corinthians 13:13

2. Harry L. Poe, *The Gospel and Its Meaning: A Theology for Evangelism and Church Growth* (Grand Rapids: Zondervan Publishing House, 1996), pp. 19-20.

3. The hardback copy on my shelf, published by Books, Inc. New York, has no publication date and sold for ninety-eight cents—almost an antique. Over forty million copies of this book have been sold.

4. An article by James F. Engel in *Christianity Today,* December 16, 1991, asked the question "Who's Really Doing Evangelism?" In a survey of 1,500 readers of the magazine (one-third clergy, almost all college graduates—not your average church members) Engel discovered that their evangelistic efforts consisted of: having spiritual discussions (33%); inviting someone to church (18%); attempts to develop friendships (11%); offering a piece of literature (8%); inviting someone to a Bible study (4%); and explaining God's plan of salvation (1%).

5. This list of passages could be quite long, but some that come to mind are Psalm 51:1-4, 10-13; Ephesians 2:4-10; 1 John 1:8-9; and a multitude of stories in both testaments of God's patience, forgiveness, and restorative love. Note especially that Jesus was known as "the friend of sinners" and full of compassion as well as the one able to provide healing and strength. And it might be especially helpful to remember Paul's admonition related to anger (Ephesians 4:23-27).

6. From the Asbury Study it is not easy to say which parental "faith modeling" activities are most important for passing on the faith, but surely a list would include: daily times of prayer together, regular reading of portions of the Bible and other Christian devotional materials, spending time talking and listening to each other about daily happenings and asking "What would Jesus do?" "What should you do?," and showing that God's love in us reaches out not only to our friends and family, but also to others in need both near and far away.

7. A national study of Protestant "marginal members" and "mental affiliates" funded by the Lilly Endowment and conducted by C. Kirk Hadaway and Penny Long Marler was reported in the *Review of Religious Research,* Vol. 35, No. 1 (September, 1993). The study discovered only 20% of active Protestant members say they had a father who "never attended," while 45% of "mental affiliates" (not church members who nevertheless attend occasionally) reported their fathers never attended.

8. A significant amount of serious sociological research on men and the church is emerging. One of the leaders in this movement is Dr. Woody Davis, Director of Evangelism and Congregational Development, East Ohio Conference of the United Methodist Church. His own research indicates one of the problems for many men in the church is the language we use. Much of it lacks any sense of adventure and a call to "come be part of the team"—both of which seem evident in Jesus' call to discipleship. Perhaps this more radical definition of love and spiritual life needs to be more of what at least men hear if they are to step forward and be counted as Christian witnesses.

9. The Marler and Hadaway study cited above revealed 77% of active Protestant adult members were also active during their last year of high school, compared to only 43% of those who were "mental affiliates" but no longer active.

10. "What a Friend We Have in Jesus," words by Joseph Scriven, ca. 1855, *The United Methodist Hymnal,* 526.

11. Koran, v and ix, as quoted in *The World Treasury of Religious Quotations,* compiled and edited by Ralph L. Woods (New York: Garland Books, 1966), p. 355.

12. See the emphasis on prayer without ceasing in Acts 12:5; Romans 1:9; 1 Thessalonians 1:3, 2:13, 5:17; 2 Timothy 1:3.

13. *Experiencing God* (Nashville: Lifeway Press, 1990) is designed to accomplish just what its title suggests. Recognizing that many in their churches settle for a "salvation decision," the authors, Southern Baptist pastors Henry T. Blackaby and Claude V. King, have created a three-month program designed to "know God in a more intimate way by experiencing God at work through you." Many thousands have discovered through this program that salvation is as much about a vital, daily, obedient relationship with God as it is about going to heaven when we die. Materials including workbooks, leaders' guides, video tapes, audio tapes and more are available through Christian bookstores or by calling 1-800-458-2772.

14. "Explaining the gospel" becomes the critical second ingredient—after modeling a relationship with God—for every group in the Asbury Study when they describe the persons who actually helped them make a decision for Christ. And the agents who are described as most important in this step of faith, especially by the youngest generations, are pastors, youth workers, and evangelists.

15. Nearly every denomination has its own "faith sharing" or "lifestyle evangelism" training program. In addition, parachurch organizations such as Net Results, the Willow Creek Association, Church Growth Institute, Child Evangelism Fellowship, Youth Specialties, Youth for Christ, Young Life, Intervarsity Christian Fellowship, Campus Crusade for Christ, The Navigators, and Evangelism Explosion all have extensive experience and resources in training persons for personal evangelism.

16. *Pray the Price* (Muncie, Ind.: Prayer Point Press, 1997), pp. 44-45.

17. Win Arn, Carroll Nyquist and Charles Arn, *Who Cares About Love: How to bring together the Great Commission and the Great Commandment* (Monrovia, Calif.: Church Growth Press, 1986), p. 119. This book could provide excellent guidance for congregations trying to learn how to be more loving.

18. An excellent new book on the spiritual development of children is *Joining Children on the Spiritual Journey: Nurturing a Life of Faith* (Grand Rapids: Baker Books, 1998) by Cathy Stonehouse.

19. *Christianity Explained* (Wayne, Penn.: 1985) was developed by Michael L. B. Bennett, an Australian Anglican, but is now being used in the U.S. Recognizing that fewer and fewer people understand basic biblical concepts, this approach seeks to do evangelism through a six-week presentation of the Gospel of Mark studied in a small group. It is led by trained lay people, either in a home or in a church setting, and intentionally seeks to eliminate pressuring or embarrassing those attending. Persons are told they are entirely free to drop out at any time with no questions asked. One pastor of a large church in Atlanta told me that previously they had used a popular approach to personal evangelism, but discovered only one in ten of those "won to Christ" ever became active in church. This more "relational" approach utilizing small groups has completely changed the readiness of converts to become deeply involved in their new life of faith. For additional information contact Scripture Union, P. O. Box 6720, Wayne, Pa. 19087-8720, Phone (610) 341-0830, FAX (610) 341-0836.

20. George Barna, "Trends That Affect Evangelism Today," *Equipping for Evangelism* (Minneapolis: World Wide Publications, 1996), pp. 211-14.

21. From "In His Time," words by D. Ball, copyright © 1984 by Maranatha! Music. Used by permission.

22. From "As the Deer Pants," words by M. Nystrom, copyright © 1978 by Maranatha! Music. Used by permission.

23. From "In Moments Like These," words by D. Graham, copyright © 1980 by C.A. Music (a division of Christian Artists Corp.), administered by Music Services.

SUBJECT INDEX

Gillespie, V. Bailey, 100, 104-5
glory, 22, 28, 39-44, 58
God
  call of, 78-79, 103
  face of, 40
  kingdom of, 45-52
  knowing, 57
  voice of, 17
Goddard, Hule, 93
good infection, 8, 25, 34, 36, 61-62, 66
gospel
  explained, 72, 75, 81, 118, 150-51
  remembered, 75, 97, 124
Griffin, James Wesley, 116
Griffin, Nancy Marsh, 111

Hadaway, C. Kirk, 173
healing, 78
Hine, Stuart, 15
holiness, 22, 44, 54, 55, 129, 131, 168
Holy Trinity, 7, 29-37, 39, 142
Howe, Neil, 112
Hundley, Smith, 159

inter-religious dialogue, 17
interview format, 162-64

James, William, 84, 104, 128
Jefferson, Thomas, 30
Jones, E. Stanley, 51, 169
judgment, 26-27

Kerr, Hugh T., 108
King, Claude V., 173
Koran, 143
K'ung-Fu-tzu, 19

Lewis, C. S., 32-36, 110
Luther, Martin, 63

McAllister, Dawson, 96
McIntosh, Gary, 172
Marler, Penny Long, 173
"Marriage Encounter," 149
medicine of life, 64
meekness, 46
Messiah, 19, 23, 42, 43, 48
Moses, 21, 40, 45, 53
Mother Teresa, 7, 95
Mulder, John M., 108
mystery, 15, 44

New Age movement, 29
new covenant, 23, 24, 52-60
Nyquist, Carroll, 154

Oden, Thomas, 166

Paul, 15, 16, 44, 106, 148, 166
Peter, 79, 150
Phillips, Tom, 110
Plato, 19
Poe, Harry L., 135
prayer, 146, 153, 173

religions, 17, 18, 61
remnant revelation, 18, 19
repentance, 23, 24, 47, 49, 56, 76
restoration, 78
revelation, 14-19
Rice, Wayne, 87

sacrament, 79, 136, 169
Sagan, Carl, 15
salvation, 19, 27, 58, 64, 136
sanctification, 56, 78, 129-30
Sarah, 19, 20
savior, 27, 43
Scriven, Joseph, 143
Sheldon, Charles, 138
Socrates, 19
Socratic evangelism, 158
Solomon, 47-48
Son of Man, 27
Starbuck, Edwin D., 85
Strauss, William, 112

Tertullian, 30, 32
Thomas, Wally, 133
training resources, 151-55, 174
transformation, 50, 61, 63-65
"Tres Dias," 120

under five decisions, 69-80
University of Michigan, 89

"Walk to Emmaus," 149, 159
Well, Don, 87
Wesley, Charles, 63, 65
Wesley, John, 62-65, 129
Withers, David, 101, 145-46
witnesses, 22
WWJD, 138

SCRIPTURE INDEX

177